Being a Girl
Who Leads

BEING A GIRL Who Leads

Becoming a leader by following Christ

SHANNON KUBIAK PRIMICERIO

BethanyHouse

MINNEAPOLIS, MINNESOTA

Being a Girl Who Leads
Copyright © 2006
Shannon Kubiak Primicerio

Cover design by Jennifer Parker

Published by Bethany House Publishers
11400 Hampshire Avenue South
Bloomington, Minnesota 55438

Bethany House Publishers is a division of
Baker Publishing Group, Grand Rapids, Michigan.

Printed in the United States of America

ISBN-13:   978-0-7642-0091-5
ISBN-10:   0-7642-0091-7

Library of Congress Cataloging-in-Publication Data

CIP data applied for

ISBN 0-7642-0091-7

To Megan Barbour
Thanks for being a girl who leads!

About the Author

Shannon Kubiak Primicerio resides in Southern California with her husband, Michael. Together the two enjoy watching baseball, playing Bocce ball, flying kites, and hanging out at the beach.

In addition to writing, Shannon speaks at youth and women's events nationwide. She has a B.A. in Journalism and a minor in Biblical Studies from Biola University and was the recipient of the *North County Times* "Excellence in Writing" award in 2000 and the San Diego Christian Writer's Guild "Nancy Bayless Award for Excellence in Writing" in 2003. She has been interviewed on radio and television programs across the nation, including PBS's *Religion and Ethics Newsweekly*. She has also been interviewed by *Time* magazine.

To learn more about Shannon, you can visit her Web site, *www.beingagirlbooks.com*, or you can e-mail her at *shannon@ beingagirlbooks.com*. She loves to hear from her readers.

Contents

Ten Lies That Are Ripping Us Off

Leadership is not a position you can step into and out of, and it has nothing to do with your age. True leadership is a conscious choice to stand for something in a world that falls for everything. Being a girl who leads means making a conscious effort to apply the Word of God to real life—no compromises. Authentic Christians follow the lead of Jesus Christ in all they do and say. Unfortunately, the world doesn't really know too much about what that looks like because Christians are compromising left and right.

Maybe we are not making huge compromises that would incriminate us if we had to stand before a judge and a jury. But if we are honest, we will admit that we are all buying into the seemingly small and harmless compromises that masquerade as pop culture. There is no such thing as a harmless compromise when it comes to morality and the standards by which you choose to govern your life. Everything in this world either glorifies God or mocks Him. Nothing is neutral. And in everything we say and do, *we* either glorify God or we mock Him. All too often Christians give in to the mockery just as much as the rest of the world does.

We don't want to be different. We would much rather compromise than stand out. Like many magazines and movies suggest, we allow ourselves to become objects and not people. Instead of focusing on who we are, we become consumed with how we look. Soon we become empty shells—pretty on the outside, hollow on the inside. For the most part, people can't tell us apart from the non-Christian girls. We dress like them, talk like them, and behave in much the same manner. There is nothing wrong with being trendy, but we haven't stopped there.

We have cloned the world and Christianized it. Little by little we have let our guard down. We think that because the sins in our lives are watered-down versions of what everyone else is doing (we will tell a lie but we won't commit murder; we will watch a movie with an explicit sex scene but we won't have premarital sex ourselves; we will disrespect our parents but we won't go out and get drunk on the weekends; etc.), then we are okay.

Without even thinking twice, we breathe in compromise like it is oxygen, and when we exhale we pollute the reputation of Jesus Christ. This is no small offense. Now, granted, everyone who reads this book is at a different place. Yet if we closely (and honestly) examine ourselves, we will all find compromise in our lives somewhere.

I used to think certain things didn't happen in the Christian community. But then I had a friend who attended a *Christian college* tell me she walked in on two classmates having sex in the *prayer chapel* in the middle of the night. That blew my theory right out of the water. Perhaps you are a little bit naïve, like I was. And maybe some of the topics in this book are not a problem for you. You must realize, though, that they are a problem in our generation, our culture, and maybe our church. It is vitally important that we treat them like the threats they are. We need to learn how to recognize subtle compromises and refuse to take part in them. We need to educate ourselves also, so we can go out and warn others about these lies that look so much like the truth.

Satan is destroying Christian testimonies everywhere, and his tools are quite good. Sure, I have met Christian girls who are experimenting with sex, drugs, alcohol, and self-mutilation. But this experimentation is not where the problem starts. The problem starts in the little things, and it builds momentum as more and more Christians buy into the world's lie that certain compromises are just part of having some harmless fun. The biggest problem among Christian girls today is that we do not want to lead—we don't think we have to. Life is too enjoyable to waste our time on things we can worry about later. We're having too much fun being girls to care about being girls who lead. And we are paying dearly for this kind of self-centered attitude.

It's time we stop being naïve or ignorant. We need to face a few issues head on and clean up some of the dirty places in our lives.

Stop being fake! Stop pretending! Sometimes I wish I could stand on my roof and scream that as loudly as I can. Other times I want to scream it as loudly as I can at the mirror. *Being a Girl Who Leads* is a book I had to write because its message is one I desperately needed to learn and apply to my life every day. When it comes to "little" compromises, I have been the biggest offender of them all. Such compromises are, unfortunately, often the hallmark of those of us who were raised in Christian homes and have never had much experience with "real sin."

Many girls just like you have come to me, either in person or via e-mail, and have opened their hearts and shared their stories with me. Some of the stories break my heart; others make my blood boil because of the mockery they are making of Christ and His sacrifice. A few make me laugh because I have been there before too, not that long ago. In a generation full of followers, many girls are looking for role models and leaders that often do not exist. It's no wonder that so many struggle, trying to find purpose and meaning in a world that tells us to look to Hollywood and MTV to find happiness. But they will never find satisfaction in anything except a relationship with Jesus Christ.

In all of the e-mails I receive and conversations I have with girls I meet, the struggles are always the same. So I have narrowed them down to ten topics—ten areas where we compromise more often than we don't. I have dedicated an entire chapter in this book to each one. The ten lies Christians girls buy into the most are:

1. You have to buy immodest clothing and vulgar music because it is "in" and there are no other choices.
2. It does not matter who your friends are or how they live their lives. Sin is relative, and what is wrong for you may not be wrong for them.
3. You should never let anyone know who you really are—your deepest fears and your biggest dreams—because they might turn around and hurt you someday.
4. It's okay to use profanity or Christian forms of profanity. They are just words. It is not a big deal.
5. Boundaries and guidelines are for goody-goodies. Freedom is what life is really about.
6. You can give your heart away to everyone you meet and remain completely unaffected by it, even when your heart gets broken.
7. Lying and gossip are not really sin—they are just artistic forms of conversation.
8. You can do everything except have sex and still be pure.
9. You can hate your parents without dishonoring God.
10. Life is all about having fun.

If Christian girls decided to ban together and fight against these ten lies, we would see an incredible revolution sweep across our generation. We would change the world as we know it. But it will only work if each of us makes a conscious and firm decision to stand up and *lead* in these areas. In case you have not noticed, we do not all live on the same block or attend the same school. So we have to work on becoming authentic together yet separately.

Make up your mind in this moment that you are going to dare to be different no matter what the cost may be. Trendy? Yeah, we can be trendy. But we cannot live for the Lord with the world in our pockets, so there will be sacrifices that will have to be made. I will talk more about that later on. It is time to be real here, so I am going to be.

You will have to forgive my brutal honesty at certain places within this book. This is a message that squeezes my heart. We cannot afford to water this one down—we have done that for long enough. There is more to life than meets the eye. Compromise is killing authentic Christianity. And there is only one way to change that: to stand up and be a girl who leads.

1

The Buck Stops Here

You have no idea how much power you really have. You think that because you are just one girl—sometimes a shy or insecure girl—you cannot make a difference or lead anyone else. But you can! Right now you have more potential to influence the lives of other people and the trends of the times than you ever will again. And you do not have power just because God has given you power; you have power because *the world* has given it to you.

According to the U.S. Census Bureau, there were fourteen million teenage girls in the United States in the year 2000. Market researchers are saying that people born between 1979 and 1994 are now the second-largest demographic group in the United States—second only to baby boomers, those who are forty to fifty-eight years old.[1]

Millions of dollars are spent every year as researchers attempt to uncover the likes and the dislikes of teenage girls. Somewhere in a nice, cushy office building there are men and women dressed in suits spending their eight-hour work days studying *you*. They want to know what you like and do not like, and how you will spend your money. If you buy it, they will make more of it until you will not buy it anymore. If you will not buy it, the trend will quickly fizzle and go off the market completely.

Market researchers are also saying that teen shoppers are not just influential in today's market. Your spending power is expected to remain strong as you get older, and your tastes will probably greatly impact the next generation.[2] What does this have to do with being a girl who leads?

It has everything to do with being a girl who leads because three of the most popular trends among teens today are music with explicit lyrics, immodest clothing, and movies with sexual content. Those things are only popular because *teenage girls just like you are buying them*.

A report issued by *Marketresearch.com* said, "Companies will need to work extra hard to keep pace with this fast-moving, heavy spending, technologically-advanced target; successful companies will listen to anticipate the needs and wants of teens in order to satisfy them."[3]

WHAT DO YOU DO WITH YOUR BUCK?

How hard do you make companies work for your buck? Do you buy into the trends of the times simply because you feel like you have to? Or do you use this incredible amount of power bestowed upon you by market researchers to influence your generation—and the next—for God's glory?

A big part of being a leader is standing against things that you know are wrong and being willing to go against the flow and be different. If you look and act like the crowd, you are part of the crowd. And if you are part of the crowd, you are not leading it. It's time for Christian girls to stand up and refuse to do something or buy something just because it's popular.

Now, I am not saying that you need to dress like your grandmother and listen only to hymns. But I am saying that you need to be wise in your decisions and how you spend your money. And let's be honest here: Most girls spend a lot of money simply trying to keep up with the latest trends.

Clothes shopping is hard. On the West Coast, in the summertime, it can seem nearly impossible. Let's pinpoint one item of clothing as an example. Bun-hugging shorts, not any bigger than a pair of underwear, line store shelves every spring and summer. They are anything but modest, and if we are honest, we will admit that they are anything but comfortable as well. Finding shorts that are long enough can be a daunting task. Trust me. I have the same problem you do.

But this year, if you refuse to buy those shorts, you just might start to change the trend, making it easier for all of us next year. *Yeah right*, you're probably thinking. *Just because I stop buying the shorts doesn't mean they will stop making the shorts.* Maybe not, if you are the only one who stops. But think of it like this: Let's say that all of the girls in the junior high and high school youth groups at your church decided not to buy clothes like that. That's a significant number of girls who shop in the same stores at the same mall who will *not* be purchasing short shorts this year. It would have enough of an impact on sales figures to get people's attention.

Let's say the girls in *all* of the local youth groups began to stop buying those clothes. That would result in hundreds or thousands (depending on where you live) of girls in junior high and high school who are no longer buying into the trend. The result? Countless stores would suffer from low sales figures, and they would be forced to send all of the unpurchased short shorts back to the warehouse. Manufacturers notice things like that and amend their lines accordingly.

In the meantime, use some scissors and cut off old pairs of jeans and wear them as shorts that *are* long enough, if you can't find anything else that works. Wear Bermuda shorts if you have to. Whatever you do, don't follow the trend of wearing super short shorts. Stick it out and refuse to give in until they change the styles.

One Person Can Make a Difference

You probably think one person alone can't do anything, but I know better. When I was in college I met a lady with a teenage daughter, and she told me about the time when they went shopping at the mall for some new school clothes. In a certain store, there was a very vulgar and explicit music video being shown while she and her daughter shopped, so this lady complained to the store manager, who rudely told her to take it up with corporate headquarters.

So she wrote a letter to corporate headquarters, telling them she was the mother of a teenage daughter and she (the mother) was involved with a women's Bible study group of about one hundred other women with teenage daughters. In her letter she explained that she and all the other women in the study were going to stop shopping there, and they were going to tell their other friends with teenage daughters to stop shopping there too if the store did not play more appropriate music and music videos while they shopped.

A few weeks later she received a written apology from corporate headquarters with the promise to change. A few weeks after that, she returned to the store with her daughter and found both the vulgar music and the vulgar music videos were gone.

After I shared this story at a mother/daughter event, a woman came up and told me that she too had great success in standing against something she thought was wrong. This particular woman was offended by some very graphic ads a certain store had facing out of their windows and into the mall. She did not want her children to be subjected to something she considered to be pornographic. So she went into the store and asked to speak to a manager, who instructed her to fill out a comment card with her complaint. Several weeks later the window displays were changed and the ads no longer faced into the mall.

Change only occurs because one person stands up somewhere and decides to change things. We do not have to tolerate much of the impropriety that is forced on us. A lot of things would change if we simply stood up and said something.

Most companies do not want to deal with the potential threat of unhappy customers, so they will change at the first hint of trouble to avoid a potential conflict that could become detrimental to their sales figures. Don't be afraid to speak up, even if the store you are dealing with is a little slower at coming around. Exercise your consumer spending power and don't buy their product if it is offensive.

Who Determines What Is "In"?

Many trends can be traced back to the one person who started it. In the late 1990s everyone wanted to have the Rachel cut. Teenage girls, myself included, spent tons of money trying to make their hair look like Jennifer Aniston's hairdo on the television show *Friends*.

A few years ago, when Jessica Simpson got married, she was photographed in a sweatshirt with the words *Soon to be Mrs. Lachey* embroidered on the back. Stores have been selling out of *Soon to be Mrs.* shirts ever since. This is not just a trend with brides. These shirts are everywhere. You know the ones I am talking about: *Soon to be Mrs. Kutcher,* or *Soon to be Mrs. Bloom.* I even saw one that said *Soon to be the next Mrs. Pitt.*

I don't think Jennifer and Jessica were trying to create cultural revolutions with their haircuts and clothing choices, but they did. And those *are not* the trends that we need to work at changing. They are just an example of how quickly trends start. There is nothing wrong with wanting to be trendy—to an extent.

But let's go back to the three most popular trends that I mentioned earlier, and let's see why we need to fight against trends like these. If Christian girls worked together on combating these three trends, they would start a cultural revolution that would greatly impact our society.

THE NAKED TRUTH ABOUT WHAT'S IN YOUR CLOSET

The first, and most common, of these trends is immodest clothing. It's everywhere. Tops are almost always too low or too see-through, and shorts and skirts are almost always too short.

Why is this a problem? Why is it that a Christian girl aspiring to be a leader—or simply aspiring to grow in her walk with the Lord—should make an effort to turn this trend around and bring modesty back into fashion?

I could go off for an entire book on this topic. But this isn't the time for that, so I will keep it simple. Let's begin by looking at what 1 Corinthians 6:19–20 says:

> Do you not know that your body is a temple of the Holy Spirit who is in you, whom you have from God, and that you are not your own? For you have been bought with a price: therefore glorify God in your body.

Glorifying God in your body does *not* mean letting the Holy Spirit reside in a body clothed—or not clothed—to resemble a Playboy playmate. If we let our cleavage pop out of our shirts and we let our cheeks fall out of our shorts, we are not glorifying God with our bodies. We're flaunting ourselves in impure and immodest ways.

You may disagree with my statement. You might say that the Bible doesn't say specifically what should and should not be covered, that it is all a matter of personal preference and people don't need to get so bent out of shape about this issue. You might even quote I Samuel 16:7, which says, "Man looks at the outward appearance, but the Lord looks at the heart."

And that is true, but your outward appearance is a reflection of the inward state of your heart. And if you want to be a leader, you need to come to terms with the fact that people are going to watch you before they will ever follow you. They *will* judge a book by its cover. Right or wrong, that's how it is. And you would not expect to find an issue of *Christianity Today* or *BRIO* magazine clothed in a *Playboy* cover.

> *Your outward appearance is a reflection of the inward state of your heart.*

First Corinthians 8:9, 12 says: "But beware lest somehow this liberty of yours become a stumbling block to those who are weak.... When you thus sin against the brethren, and wound their weak conscience, you sin against Christ" (NKJV). And who are those with a weak conscience when it comes to immodesty? The guys who surround us—Christians and non-Christians alike.

Give the Guys a Break

Let me tell you, guys are wired differently. I didn't realize just how differently until I was married. When I dated my husband, and while we were engaged, I took great care to dress modestly. But once we were married, I felt the freedom to walk around the house in house clothes (small shorts and shirts that show a little midriff). One day as I was cleaning the house, he happened to mention how good he thought I looked in one of my little outfits. So I used that moment as a launching pad for what really goes on in a guy's head. And my dear, sweet husband admitted that seeing something as simple as a little skin is a huge turn-on for a guy.

Perhaps some of us don't realize this. We look in the mirror and think "cute," while the guys look at us and think "naked." But more often than not, I'm going to bet that we *do know* what immodest clothing does to the guys around us—and we like the attention.

Face it, when a guy is attracted to you or me, he becomes like putty in our hands. He is suddenly willing to do anything for us, and he is constantly flattering us as he tells us how good we look. Who doesn't like that kind of attention? But the honest truth is that when we use our bodies to get that kind of attention, we turn ourselves into objects of lust and we dishonor God and ourselves. The Bible's idea of true beauty is found in modesty.

In Genesis 24 we read about the first time Isaac, Abraham's son, and Rebekah met. Under his master's instruction, Abraham's servant went out searching for a bride for Isaac. As he was returning with her, she saw a man out in the distance and asked the servant if he was the one who was to be her husband.

When he said yes, Genesis 24:65 tells us that Rebekah took her veil and *covered* herself. Verse 67 tells us that Isaac *loved* her. Rebekah honored God, herself, and Isaac with her modesty, and the end result was a husband who *loved* her, not a man who *lusted* after her. She did not have to take it all off to win his attention or his affection.

Eye-Candy

When we dress immodestly, we let ourselves become eye-candy (whether it's intentional or not) for our brothers in Christ and any other guys we see. Like I said earlier, we become objects of lust. We degrade who God has made us, and we cause others to stumble as a result.

I surveyed a group of *Christian* teen boys who regularly attend youth group and asked them what they thought of girls who wear immodest clothing. One fifteen-year-old boy said it makes him think about sex. One seventeen-year-old boy said it makes him think that the girl's body is all she has to offer, and he would "pity" her. Another boy simply said it would make him think the girl was easy.

Guys just think differently than we do. They are visual creatures. None of us want to be cheapened by guys who will undress us with their eyes or think we are easy. It's just not honoring to God, and it doesn't do much for our self-esteem either. Even godly guys have a problem with lust. So do yourself—and the guys around you—a favor and cover up.

As we strive to be girls who lead, modesty will become a bigger and bigger issue for us. For those of us who want to lead others, the bar is set higher. I struggle just as much as you do. Recently my husband and I went to visit my grandparents, and I wore a new white shirt under a cardigan sweater.

I was certainly not trying to be immodest. I mean, come on, I was going to see my grandparents. After we were already there, Michael pulled me aside and told me my shirt was very see-through in the sunlight. He thought it would be best if I didn't wear it again unless I wore it as an undershirt that would be completely covered up.

I could have gotten angry with him for telling me this. I could have argued that it was a new shirt and I should be able to wear it if I want to. But I realized that I am in a leadership role—I write books and speak on modesty all of the time. And so I needed to conform to what I taught to others. I took my cute new shirt and relegated it to the "undershirts only" pile.

This experience didn't make me mad; I chalked it up to the cost of being a leader. A lot of times, as leaders and outspoken Christians, we have to come to terms with the fact that there are things we shouldn't wear and things we shouldn't do simply because *other people are looking to us to be the example and set the standard.*

Modesty is one of those issues that matters in our Christian walk. So you've really got to decide: Are you going to attempt to turn the trends for God's glory, or are you going to keep going with the flow because it's easier and not that big of a deal to you?

GARBAGE IN, GARBAGE OUT

Another trend we need to look at reversing is that of music with explicit lyrics (meaning music containing profanity and other degrading language). Now, if you are like me, music is somewhat of a big deal to you. I grew up appreciating music. My dad is a big music fan and likes a lot of classic rock stuff. When I was growing up we would play "Guess the Song" or "Who is This?" on long car rides. When a song came on the radio, we would have a contest to see who could name the song and the artist quickest, after listening to only the first few chords of the song.

As Christians, we need to be careful in choosing what music we listen to because music sets the mood. It sets the tone for our day. It sticks in our heads. If you are like me, you pick music that matches your mood. When you're happy, you listen to happy songs. When you are bummed out, you listen to depressing music. When you are in love, you listen to love songs. Sometimes you even listen to the same song over and over again. Certain memories are linked to certain songs. A good day has even been known to sour quickly due to a sad or angry song on the radio.

Most Christians can probably quote more song lyrics than Bible verses. If we let explicit music get into our minds and hearts, it will cloud our thoughts and influence our behavior. Explicit music isn't the only music we need to be cautious about; we also need to be careful of music that is very sexual in nature.

If you and your boyfriend (or even a guy friend) are in a car and a song comes on the radio with lyrics that say something about "making love to you" or "doing it all night long," what do you think you are going to start thinking about? What do you think *he* is going to start thinking about? Guys have a hard enough time with that stuff already.

Philippians 4:8 says:

> Whatever is true, whatever is honorable, whatever is right, whatever is pure, whatever is lovely, whatever is of good repute, if there is any excellence and if anything worthy of praise, dwell on these things.

That's hard to do if your minds are full of profanity and sexual thoughts. You might not think music affects you that much. When I was in junior high I didn't either. I wasn't walking with the Lord yet (although I called myself a Christian), and I borrowed a CD with a parental advisory warning on it from a friend. *Thirteen years later* I still remember those explicit and vulgar lyrics. Sometimes they come to my mind for no reason at all. Music is made to be catchy. It is made to stick with you.

You do not have to buy a CD just because it is popular. If you stand against it because it is something that could cloud your mind or make you think about inappropriate things, then maybe others will stand against it too. Be the leader. Show others there is an alternative. Be the change you want to see here.

Perhaps you will start a new trend and change what's "in" and what's not. That hit song won't be a hit anymore if the CD stops selling. Some girls in a Bible study I used to teach even suggested getting together to call secular radio stations and vote for the weekly top forty. They figured if Christians voted, the top songs might be different. Even if you don't reverse the trend, at least you won't be clouding your own mind. A good test about whether or not you should be listening to a certain CD is found in whether you would be comfortable getting in the car with your parents—or one of your youth leaders—and blaring that CD full blast.

A real leader goes the extra mile to keep her heart pure and her mind focused on the things of the Lord.

"Be Careful Little Eyes What You See"

One more area I want to address is that of movies and television shows with latent sexual content. Too many movies make light of premarital sex, extramarital sex, and gay and lesbian relationships. Those are not funny issues. They are not small issues. They are *sin* issues.

And I'll be honest with you. For a part of my college years I spent Thursday nights glued to my television, wanting to know what was going to happen next in the lives of Ross, Rachel, Monica, Chandler, Phoebe, and Joey. It was a show that defined our times, and I was a *Friends* fan.

My friend "Cheryl" was one of my only friends who stood opposed to the show. She pointed out all of the things that were morally and biblically wrong with the lives of the characters. But we wore her down over time, claiming that "it just isn't that big of a deal." Pretty soon she was more into the show than the rest of us. And eventually she began to live her life like some of the characters.

She got caught up in a bad relationship with some smooth-talking Romeo. When we tried to warn her of certain dangers, her response was, "You watched the characters on *Friends* do it for years, and you thought it was okay. So don't talk to me about why you think it's wrong in my life."

What she was doing wasn't right, but she had a point. Looking back, I would have easily and gladly given up the years of watching *Friends* if I knew how badly it was hurting someone who really was one of my friends.

Television shows and movies wear down our resolve just as much as our own peers do. As girls, we find ourselves getting emotionally attached to characters on shows or the actors and actresses who portray them, and we begin to follow their lead in how they live their lives. Maybe not all the way, but we sure get close to that line. Some of us even begin to follow the personal lives of our favorite actors and actresses and are devastated when their marriages fall apart. We might go so far as to be able to name their favorite ice cream flavors and every movie they have ever been in.

As we get caught up in their personal lives, we also get wrapped up in the stories that drive movies and television programs. One awful result of this is we may find ourselves *wanting* people in the story to sin. We fall in love with certain characters and develop some sort of one-sided relationship with them. We want to see them succeed and prosper, no matter what that means. In college my friends and I wanted to see Ross and Rachel get back together so badly that we didn't care if they had sex. It was Ross and Rachel . . . so it just *seemed* right. How sad is that? We abandoned all sense of morality just to see two fictitious people get together.

If we are not careful, those very same immoralities that seem right in the lives of fictional characters will seem right in our own lives as well. Sin subtly creeps into our lives through the media in areas we think "just aren't that big of a deal."

It goes back to Philippians 4:8. We've got to be thinking about what is true and pure, what really is right and wrong, and not just what "feels" or "seems" right and wrong in that setting.

COMPROMISE IS A LEADER KILLER

As Christian girls we have real power. We have the potential to influence society and set a new standard for what's "in" and what's not. Yet all too often we settle somewhere in the middle, compromising our standards for the sake of popularity. And instead of emerging as strong leaders, we come out as dwarfed Christians.

We think we can still be Christians and dress however we want, listen to whatever we want, and watch whatever we want. And we *can*. But it doesn't mean we *should*. If we give in to those things, we will not be strong Christians, growing Christians, or set-apart Christians that are leaders in our generation.

Recently I was having a conversation with a girl I know. She's a strong Christian and someone I would consider to be a leader. But she had done something she really shouldn't have, and then she lied about it. She told me that she woke up the next morning to have her quiet time with the Lord and found that she just couldn't read her Bible or pray until she repented and came clean.

Sin and compromise will always block our access to God. Not because He has turned His back on us, but because we have turned our backs on Him. We've said, "I don't want to do it *your* way. I'd much rather do it *my* way."

It's been said that a Christian can do the most for the world when she is the least like it. If you want to be a leader, you've got to be different. Sometimes you need to give up a few things—popular and trendy things—for the sake of the kingdom. This is not a popular message, I know.

> *A Christian can do the most for the world when she is the least like it.*

But as I prayed about the concept of being a girl who leads, a certain man came to my mind. We know him as the rich young ruler. His story is told in Matthew, Mark, and Luke. I find it fascinating that we are not told his name, yet we are told three things about him.

He was rich: he had everything his heart could have ever wanted. He had everything but Jesus, and he still was not satisfied.

He was young: perhaps too young to realize that it is better to cling to Jesus and let go of everything else than to cling to everything else and let go of Jesus. I wonder if a rich *old* ruler would have made the same mistake.

He was a ruler: he had authority and power. He could do anything he wanted. He was his own boss, and he answered to no one—except Jesus alone, and this man didn't like what Jesus had to say.

He asked Jesus what he had to do to obtain eternal life. Jesus told him to keep the commandments. This man said he had kept all of the commandments but was still found lacking. So Jesus answered him in Matthew 19:21, saying:

> If you wish to be complete, go and sell your possessions and give to the poor, and you will have treasure in heaven; and come, follow Me.

The Bible tells us that the rich young ruler went away grieved because he had a lot of stuff. Maybe you have been reading this and fighting me on why you need to attempt to change these trends. Perhaps you want Jesus, but you also want your immodest clothing, your explicit CDs, and your sexually-laden movies and TV shows.

For a while I counseled every week with a girl who told me she believed in Jesus, but she still wanted to party. Like the rich young ruler, she went away sorrowful every week. She would sit before me with mascara running down her cheeks as she cried. She knew she wasn't happy—yet she wanted to party more than she wanted to fellowship with Jesus.

Although you can have Jesus while having all of those other things (since salvation is free), you will not grow that way. Growth is costly and leading is hard. The same Jesus that told the rich young ruler to sell all that he had just might be speaking to you as well.

Give up these things, and step up and lead, He is saying. *Change the trends. Leave a mark on your generation. Be a leader. Follow only me.*

It only takes one person to start a trend or spark a major change in pop culture. You've been given the power to be that one person. Are you going to use it? Or are you going to waste it? Are you going to step up and be a leader? Or are you going to sit back and do nothing as your generation continues to lead the next generations astray?

You've been presented with a choice. You cannot put this book down and be undecided. To say that you're going to think about it means that you have decided not to step up and lead. You know the right thing to do. You even know what God is *calling* you to do.

The next time someone comes to you in an attempt to get you to buy into one of the latest trends that you know isn't right, simply look them in the eye and calmly (and nicely) say, "The buck stops here." Then start to implement a change.

FOR FURTHER THOUGHT:

1. What are some of the latest trends that have taken over your school or your youth group that you know are not honoring to God?

2. What are some of the trends that you tend to wrestle with and give in to most?

3. Why are these things appealing to you?

4. Do you know anyone who stands against some popular trends because she believes the trends are wrong? How is this person viewed by others? How do you view her?

5. What are some practical ways you can stand against pop culture when it is wrong?

LEADERSHIP IN ACTION:

Keep a log for the next month of all of the things you spend your money on. Be specific. Don't just write "Bought CD." Write "Bought Jars of Clay CD for $15." If you buy clothing, specify exactly what you bought.

At the end of the month, look at how you spent your money and see if you regret any of your purchases. Did you see a movie that turned out to be gross and vulgar? Did you buy a shirt that shrank after just one wash and was no longer wearable? Look for ways you can become wiser in your spending habits and refuse to buy something just because it is popular.

Notes

1. "It's A Teen Thing," *Look-Look*, *www.look-look.com/looklook/html/ Test_Drive_Press_WWD4.html* (accessed May 23, 2005).

2. Ibid.

3. *Mintel International Group, Ltd., www.marketresearch.com/product/display.asp ?productid=1078092&SID=78467729_318991978_397294843 &kw=teen* (accessed May 23, 2005).

2

In Bad Company

When my friend "Missy" was sixteen, she worked at a local hole-in-the-wall snack shop. It was her first job, and in the beginning she loved it. After she had been there for quite some time, she asked me to pray for her because some Christians she worked with (people she knew from youth group) were putting her in an awkward position. When the boss wasn't around and there weren't any customers, they would go into the back room and do things they really shouldn't be doing.

Some were compromising their purity; others were simply being dishonest. Another person was doing drugs. Missy finally decided to talk to some of them about their behavior. They admitted to doing all of these things, but they didn't see anything wrong with them. They thought she was just being a killjoy.

Several days after Missy told me this shocking and horrible news, she called me to tell me she had quit her job, even though she had worked there longer than anyone else. When I got her message, something inside of me cheered. Finally, someone got it. After confronting her co-workers about their sinful behavior and seeing they had no intention of changing, Missy decided to quit her job rather than stay on in a compromising situation.

She sent a very loud and clear signal that said, "I don't think what you are doing is okay." When she quit, she told her boss there were some things going on that she didn't think were appropriate, but she left the details for her boss to figure out on her own. She didn't gossip about the others; she wasn't a tattletale. She simply confronted her co-workers face-to-face and then left when they said they would not change because they did not see anything wrong with what they were doing. A few weeks later God blessed her with an even better job at Starbucks.

To me, Missy stands out as an example of a true leader. Why? Because she did not leave herself in a situation where she could have eventually been worn down and led to compromise. She didn't stay and try to remain popular among those who were involved in life-styles of sin. She was bold enough to stand up to them, and she didn't care what they thought of her for it. I probably would have been a lot more timid than Missy.

> *The people we spend our time with have a great influence on our lives.*

Many of us make a critical mistake when we think we can surround ourselves with people who do not have the same moral standards we do and not be affected by them. The people we spend our time with have a great influence on our lives. Whether it is at work, school, or just casually hanging out, we will become like those with whom we surround ourselves.

That is why it is vitally important that we understand that Christianity is not a religion—it is a personal relationship with Jesus Christ. We cannot go to church on Sunday and live however we want to throughout the rest of the week, thinking we have paid our dues to God. We need to be the same girl Monday through Saturday that we are on Sunday morning. For most of us, this can become a problem if we choose the wrong type of friends.

When I think of someone who chose his friends wisely, Daniel always comes to my mind. In Daniel 1:8 it tells us, "Daniel made up his mind that he would not defile himself with the king's choice food or with the wine which he drank." As Daniel was held in exile in a foreign land, he decided not to partake in their pagan practices. He wasn't going to worship their gods or party with the natives. This decision would have been extremely difficult for him had he surrounded himself with those who *were* eating the king's choice food and drinking his wine. In fact, I would venture to guess that Daniel would have eventually given in and become just like the rest of them. The phrase "everybody's doing it" pulls a lot more weight than most of us want to admit. Daniel knew that God wanted to use him to change Babylon, so he aspired to be a leader and to be set apart. He selected as his closest friends other young Hebrew men named Hananiah, Mishael, and Azariah (also known in Scripture as Shadrach, Meschach, and Abed-nego).

As the story goes on, we find out that these four men banned together and decided to take on Babylon as they stood for the kingdom of God. They refused to compromise. They would not bow down to idols, and they continued to pray to God as they always had. Daniel survived the lion's den, and Shadrach, Meschach, and Abed-nego lived through the fiery furnace and emerged without even being singed.

Their integrity and willingness to live out their faith with no regard to the cost of disobeying the pagan king caused both King Nebuchadnezzar *and* King Darius (at different times and on different occasions) to eventually proclaim God as the one true God and to offer up praise to Him. What a legacy they left behind! They had an extraordinary amount of faith and an unusual bond of friendship. You don't see any competition between them—just a bond of unity. When Daniel got promoted by the king, he requested Shadrach, Meschach, and Abed-nego be promoted as well (Daniel 2:48–49).

Imagine what would happen on your school campus, your dance squad, or your softball team (or whatever it is you do) if you and *one* other solid Christian friend decided to stand together against compromise. The results could be radical. They would be even more radical if your circle of solid Christian friends continued to grow.

Backing Each Other Up

In college I went on a mission trip with a group of students from my university. One night, my friend Sarah got into a conversation about her purity ring with a group of guys who were about our age. I overheard them trying to sway her opinion and make her think she was missing out on some fun. I knew she wasn't in danger of compromising her standards, but I also understood how desperately she wanted to communicate her passion for what she believed. So I jumped into the conversation and the two of us together gave a pretty convincing argument for why sex is something that needs to remain within the confines of marriage. When we left, the guys were scratching their heads and seemed to be seriously considering the points we had made.

Sarah and I were stronger together than either of us would have been on our own. But imagine how Sarah would have felt if I had joined the conversation and taken the other side (which I *never* would have done). She would have felt abandoned, betrayed, and maybe even a little embarrassed. We need friends who are going to stand behind us and beside us, supporting us in our decision to live for the Lord in all things. Simply put, we need friends who are going to back us up. Ecclesiastes 4:9–10 says:

Two are better than one because they have a good return for their labor. For if either of them falls, the one will lift up his companion. But woe to the one who falls when there is not another to lift him up.

At this point in your life you likely spend more time with your friends than you do with your own family. That's okay, as long as your friends are people who are going to encourage you to make wise choices and are living godly lives themselves. However, that does not mean you need to shun those who do not know the Lord and who are desperately searching for truth.

FRIENDSHIP AS BOTH MINISTRY AND MISSION

Rick Warren says every Christian is designed to have a ministry to the church and a mission to the world.[1] Perhaps part of your mission to the world is to reach those at your school or on your team who do not know the Lord. Friendship evangelism is very effective, but it is also very tricky. I went to public school from kindergarten through high school. Trust me, I know how tricky it can get. It only got harder for me as I got older, and my senior year in high school was probably the hardest year of my life to that point. Many of my Christian friends had graduated and gone to college. The only friends I had left were not saved and had no desire to be (except for a few who said they were Christians but lived an opposite lifestyle). Most of them had been simply classmates and acquaintances of mine prior to that year. We had never been close, until circumstances threw us together.

The more time I spent with them, the more I wanted to be accepted by them. Every time the hot non-Christian guys flirted with me, I found that I wanted it to happen more and more. I was having fun at school for the first time in a long time. I was always an Advanced Placement student, so school was hard work, but for the first time there was electricity to it that made it exciting. Eventually I found myself wanting to hang out with these people *all* the time.

That wasn't really a bad thing—after all, I was gaining popularity my senior year in high school. Nothing wrong with that, right? There was nothing wrong with it in theory; it all sounded good. But considering the lifestyles of some of my new friends, there were warning bells going off left and right. They partied, some drank, some slept around, and some even did drugs. Most of them swore like truck drivers. I didn't want to see these things, but I could not ignore them.

During my senior year, my previous three years of being an authentic Christian were being put to the test. My reputation was on the line. Looking back, I wish I had been stronger. But thankfully, by God's grace, I finally realized what I was doing before I gave in to total compromise.

My biggest mistake was that I began to play into the lie of relativism. I let my friends think their lifestyle was not okay for me, but it was just fine for them. I was like a Christian flashlight—I was shining brightly everywhere but at school. For some reason or another I seemed to hit my Off button whenever these people were around. I would not do the things they would do, but I didn't let them know of my disapproval for their behavior. In many respects, what I *was* doing was just as bad as what I *wasn't*. But wrong is wrong no matter who is doing it. Even when we do not feel comfortable verbally telling someone their actions are wrong, we need to make sure that we aren't verbally affirming them either.

Sometimes when my friends would tell me they had gone to a party where there was drinking involved, I would make a casual comment like "Oh, that's nice." I never should have done that.

Confronting non-Christians on their behavior is completely different than confronting others who say they are saved, because those who don't know Christ have a completely different sense of right and wrong than we do. Sure, the things they are doing *are* still wrong, but they don't have the same convictions about them that we do. First Corinthians 5:9–13 speaks to this issue:

> I have written you in my letter not to associate with sexually immoral people—not at all meaning the people of this world who are immoral, or the greedy and swindlers, or idolaters. In that case you would have to leave this world. But now I am writing you that you must not associate with anyone who calls himself a brother but is sexually immoral or greedy, an idolater or a slanderer, a drunkard or a swindler. With such a man do not even eat. What business is it of mine to judge those outside the church? Are you not to judge those inside? God will judge those outside. "Expel the wicked man from among you" (NIV).

Halfway into my senior year I began to see what was happening, so I pulled back from my unsaved friends. I didn't really have to offer an explanation as to why I couldn't come around as much. They knew I was a Christian; I had shared my faith with them numerous times. They knew where I stood, and they held to different beliefs and morals. So the best thing for me was to simply part ways with them or put a lot of space between us. There was no need for a confrontation—their lifestyle choices were between them and God. They didn't have to answer to me about them.

Years later I had a good Christian friend who was supposed to be in my wedding. She began to make some poor decisions before finally walking away from God. For a while I let it go, only offering an occasional chiding because I wanted to keep things peaceful in the weeks leading up to my wedding. But one night I couldn't hold it in anymore; I confronted her on a lot of things she was doing that were flat-out sin.

Two weeks before my wedding, she backed out of being a bridesmaid and hasn't replied to an e-mail or a letter from me since. The difference in this situation was that I couldn't hold my non-saved friends accountable to a belief system they did not claim as their own. My Christian friend, however, knew the truth and was simply ignoring it for a season of "fun and experimentation." I needed to hold her accountable to the truth she had chosen to proclaim.

After I stopped hanging out with my non-Christian friends, they noticed the ways that I was different from them, and they wanted to know why. People took note that I didn't attend wild parties, and the guys knew that none of them had ever been with me in an intimate way. To them, it seemed I was the only one "missing out" and didn't have any regrets about it. This piqued their curiosity.

Doors flew open for me to share my faith. Many of my unsaved friends kept coming back to me with countless questions. This went on even into college. I would get phone calls from time to time from old classmates and friends who were not Christians. They wanted to know if I was still holding fast to my beliefs and if I thought God could love them too.

In high school I took a handful of friends to church or youth camp and saw a few come to Christ. Sadly, though, I saw more strong Christians fall away than non-Christians come to Christ. First Corinthians 15:33 says: "Do not be deceived: 'Bad company corrupts good morals.'" I think the first four words in that sentence are the most powerful. *Do not be deceived.* That means it is not going to look like our unsaved friends, or friends who say they are saved but do not act like it, are going to bring us down. In the end, though, what the Bible says is true.

I described it to a girl I counsel in this way: If you were standing on a chair and your friend was standing below you, which of you would have an easier time getting the other person to stand next to them? Would it be easier for you to pull your friend up or for your friend to pull you down?

We cannot argue with logic and the law of gravity on that one. And sin is even stronger than gravity. It's enticing. But that's not what is alarming. The scary thing about sin is that it is subtle. It creeps into our lives through radio speakers and movie screens, and it comes out of our own mouths before we even realize it.

Having a mission to the world is a very important thing. But having your feet firmly planted on the rock of Jesus Christ is far more important. When you think you are your strongest, you are more susceptible to falling than you have ever been. In high school, a girl from youth group and I were talking about how grieved we were that another girl in the youth group got pregnant. The girl I was talking with said she knew she would never fall into sin like that, so I gently reminded her that she needed to be even more careful to make wise decisions because she felt she was above falling. She laughed my remark off at the time, but two years later she too had given in to sexual sin.

YOU ARE NOT AS STRONG AS YOU THINK

The argument I hear most often from girls who want to justify their compromises is that "Jesus dined with tax collectors and sinners. How is what I am doing any different from Him?" There are not enough pages in this entire book to explain all of the ways our situations are different than Jesus' were. But one difference stands out above the rest to me. It is this: Jesus *dined* with tax collectors and sinners. He simply sat down and shared a meal and a table with them. He didn't go out with the tax collectors when they were stealing from people. He did not join the prostitutes on the street corners of their harlotry. He did not meet them in the middle of their sinful acts, although they were living sinful lifestyles when He spent time with them. Jesus always met them on *neutral ground*. That is where He ministered to them.

During my senior year of high school, I put the same principle into practice once I realized I was starting to compromise. I would go out to eat or to a school football game with my unsaved friends; I would even have them over to my house. But I wouldn't party with them and I wouldn't join them in several other ventures where I knew bad things would be taking place. I was even cautious about when I went to their houses, paying careful attention to whether or not their parents would be home and what was planned for our time together.

Neutral ground was where I made my biggest impact with unbelievers.

It was a much safer way to share my faith with them and to love them as people without embracing their lifestyles. That is where real friendships with these people were formed. We would talk honestly, and they would ask me about my beliefs. Neutral ground was where I made my biggest impact with unbelievers. It proved to be effective. But my Christian friends who thought they could go to raging parties and shine their lights there, right in the middle of all of the drugs, sex, and alcohol, found out that it just doesn't work like that.

One by one, strong Christian after strong Christian, they would give in to sin, quoting Paul's verse about becoming "all things to all men" (1 Corinthians 9:22). That is *not* what Paul meant. If people cannot tell you are a Christian by your actions, then you are not really being effective in your mission to the world. If people cannot see that you are any different from them, there will be no reason for them to ever change. You must show people that you think Jesus Christ is far more valuable than popularity or a Friday night party. Remember, you might be the only Bible some people ever read. What message are you giving them?

Safely Sharing Our Faith

If you are going to publicly proclaim that you are a Christian, then be sure you are giving an *accurate portrayal* of what the gospel is and isn't. Yes, the gospel extends grace for sinners. But you will also be able to recognize Christians by the fruit in their lives. Don't let your fruit become rotten just so you can attempt to relate to other rotten fruit. Don't downplay your beliefs and the depth of your relationship with the Lord just so you can be accepted in a certain group of friends.

If you truly love the Lord, you will want to be surrounded by others who love Him too. Be wise and remember to practice the rule of meeting your unsaved friends on neutral (and common) ground. And please, for your own sake, make sure you have some solid Christian friends as well. Don't put yourself in a situation where you are the only solid Christian in your group. If you do, you will get worn down really fast. If you do not have any solid Christian friends, pray and ask God to bring you at least one such friend. And be open for Him to bring you one you might not expect.

An eighth-grader I know came to me because she was having problems with friends at school. Her friends said they were Christians, but they did not talk or act like it when they were at school.

They were mean and vicious, and she desperately needed to get away from them because she had been the focal point of their attacks for several months. I asked her if there were any other girls in her class. At first she said no. When I gave her a quizzical look and questioned her further, she finally admitted the truth.

There *were* other girls she could hang out with—they just weren't as popular. Many times, whether it is a conscious decision or not, we naturally gravitate toward those we think are popular and pretty. Something about their status appeals to us and we are drawn in. We don't care if they are not always nice and if their lifestyles are a little out of hand. We are blinded by the bright lights of popularity, and before we know it, we have sold our souls for something that leaves us feeling miserable.

That's where my sweet eighth-grade friend found herself. She felt beaten up and betrayed by these popular girls who befriended her; but even in the midst of her pain and rejection, the magnetic pull toward them was still there. She didn't want to make new friends—she wanted to be accepted by *these* friends. So I sat down with her and made a list of why she wanted to be friends with these girls and how she had been hurt by them in the past. The bad list far outweighed the good list. Showing it to her on paper helped a lot.

Next, I asked her to think about how she felt when people treated her like she was unpopular and unwanted. Then I had her think about how she felt when someone reached out to her and welcomed her in. I encouraged her to *be* the friend she desperately wanted to have and to reach out to the other girls in her class who had far less risqué lifestyles and lived like Christians should.

A surprising thing happened: She made some new friends and began to have fun without feeling so much pressure to be accepted. When her old friends began to bad-mouth her in the bathroom, one of her new friends stood up in her defense. By removing herself from a situation that was less than ideal, my friend found the one thing she really wanted—acceptance and true friendship. She decided popularity wasn't all that great after all.

You can never be too cautious when it comes to removing yourself from questionable friends. It might cost you something (you might find yourself down a bridesmaid, like I did), but that is far better than having to deal with the consequences that a sinful "good time" might force you to pay later on down the line. The bottom line is that none of us are as strong as we think we are. None of us will be able to withstand the pressures of our friends if we continually put ourselves in compromising situations.

We are going to do ourselves a lot of good if we *underestimate* ourselves here rather than *overestimate* what we can withstand and still be true to Christ. It's better to be too careful than not careful enough, because one big slipup is all it takes to change your entire life.

In high school I knew a girl who was a leader in the Christian club at school. She was one of the biggest and brightest witnesses on campus. Over time, though, she let her guard down, and within her first year out of high school she got pregnant. This event changed her whole world. Although I never talked to her about it, I'm pretty sure she had assumed it would never happen to her. I've met a lot of girls who thought that once.

The best thing you can do is remind yourself that it *can* happen to you. You can fall quickly and hard if you are not careful. Do yourself a favor. Meet those you want to befriend and share your faith with. Surround yourself with other Christians and look for someone who will back you up in the good decisions you are making.

Don't condemn those who are living sinful lifestyles, but don't condone their activities either. There *is* a right and wrong. It's the same for everybody, and it's very black and white. You know the right things to do, so do them. And forget about what others are going to say about you. Forget about what others are doing. The Bible, which is the absolute foundation of truth, tells us bad company *will* corrupt good morals. What kind of company have you been keeping lately?

FOR FURTHER THOUGHT:

1. Name a compromising situation you have found yourself in (or close to) recently. How did you respond? What would you do differently next time?

2. Why do you think the Bible warns us not to be deceived when it comes to the company we keep? How have you been deceived in the past?

3. How can you prevent yourself from being deceived when it comes to how close you should allow yourself to get with some of your friends?

4. Have you felt yourself being drawn in by the magnetic pull of popularity? Why do you think popularity is so appealing?

5. Examine those you know. Have you seen more Christians fall into sin by befriending the unsaved or more unsaved people come to Christ through their Christian friends? Why do you think that is?

LEADERSHIP IN ACTION:

If you have unsaved friends, closely examine the activities you participate in together. Have you established a firm distinction between what is right and wrong, or do you have an "anything goes" mentality when it comes to the lifestyles of your friends? Try finding neutral ground. Meet for coffee or a bite to eat. Or be bold like my friend Missy and leave a situation that you know may eventually cause you to compromise.

If you do not have any non-Christian friends, spend some time praying for Christians who do. Ask the Lord to make them wise in the activities and situations in which they find themselves.

Notes

1. Rick Warren, *The Purpose Driven Life* (Grand Rapids: Zondervan, 2002), 229.

3

This Isn't a Costume Party

"Who *are* you?" I studied her face as I asked the question. Her long blond hair was familiar, and there was something in her eyes that I recognized. But the expression on her face was new to me. Leaning in to study her, I squinted to try to get a better look at the girl standing before me. Turning away from the mirror, I put my head in my hands and sat on the lid of the toilet, muttering something about not knowing who I was anymore. This was a regular occurrence that began when I entered my senior year of high school and followed me into my early twenties. In fact, it happened again just this morning.

We all have these moments. Waking up one morning with a fresh resolve to be a leader, we are disheartened by day's end when we realize something has gone wrong with our plan. At first, we cannot put our finger on it. But as days and weeks go by, it becomes clear to us: In moments that mattered, we chose to step back instead of step up. Instead of daring to be different, boldly standing for what is right, we put on a mask and became just like everyone else.

You know the moments I am talking about. Someone at school is telling a dirty joke or is divulging details of a sinful weekend, and everyone else laughs and accepts what is going on. Instead of speaking up or removing yourself from the situation, you paint a smile on your face and echo their laughter. Or when those around you begin to gossip, you jump right in without hesitation, offering the juiciest piece of gossip you know.

In high school, all of the girls in my group of friends had a massive crush on a guy named "Josh Jenkins." It was so bad that our guy friends began to dress like him or imitate him just to give us a hard time. Sometimes they would yell things out as he walked by.

I would gush and swoon every time he passed by in an attempt to fit in with everyone else. One day, one of our guy friends yelled out a comment about my having a crush on Josh just as Josh himself walked by. He turned and looked my direction and kind of smirked. I was so embarrassed, and in my head I was thinking, *If only you guys knew. I don't even think he is that attractive—I am just doing this to fit in!* Later, when I tried to explain that I didn't really think Josh was attractive, all of my friends didn't believe it. They blamed my remarks on embarrassment and denial.

Whether or not I found Josh Jenkins to be attractive is not really important; it never was. But the *principle* behind my behavior is something that could have been very dangerous if I had let it creep into other areas of my life. What if my friends were smoking or drinking or stealing things from the mall? Would I have done those things too, just to fit in? I would like to say no, but every time I think of Josh Jenkins, I remember how desperately I wanted to fit in.

A SQUARE PEG IN A ROUND HOLE

My husband and I grew up in the same town but attended rival high schools. We had several mutual friends, and we apparently attended some of the same events. But we never met until I was out of college. It's a good thing, or shall I say God thing, since we both had our fair share of identity crises. We were both Christians who were solidly walking with the Lord, but we both desperately wanted to be popular.

Car and truck clubs were big things for the guys where we grew up. Guys who drove similar automobiles would form a group of sorts, and they would hang out and obsess over their cars or trucks. Many of them would have custom stickers made to go across the front of their windshields, spelling out their club name.

My husband didn't belong to a car or truck club, so he had a sticker made that said *Church Boy* in big bold letters. He and his baseball buddies used to drive around in their trucks, bumping loud music in an attempt to show others how cool they were. Oddly enough, the music he played did not fit with the slogan on his car. Although he knew he was different from the popular crowd, he still wanted to fit in with them. So he imitated their choice of music. Like a square peg trying to fit in a round hole, Michael just didn't fit in that crowd no matter how much he wanted to or how hard he tried.

My guess is that although car clubs may be foreign to you, attempting to fit in is not. You would much rather fit in than stand out, and you would rather follow than lead, if following guaranteed you a spot in the "in" crowd.

In an attempt to convince others to like us, we often become someone we are not. Somehow we miss the startling truth that other people will never be able to tell us who we really are. Sure, they can hand us a mask and tell us to have some fun, but this isn't a costume party—this is real life. You only get one shot at it. You were made to be somebody, and not just anybody. You were made to be you!

> *Other people will never be able to tell us who we really are.*

It's in Christ that we find out who we are and what we are living for. Long before we first heard of Christ . . . he had his eye on us, had designs on us for glorious living, part of the overall purpose he is working out in everything and everyone (Ephesians 1:11–12 THE MESSAGE).

On days when we feel like misfits—like square pegs trying to force our way into round holes (which is impossible, by the way)—we need to remember that there is One who made us, and *He* knows for what purposes He made us. If we don't seem to fit with a certain group of people or in a certain place, maybe it's because we are not supposed to be there. Perhaps there is something—and someone—better for us than what we have chosen for ourselves.

We live with limited vision and skewed perspective. Sometimes the things that seem like the absolute best to us are anything but. In times like this, God knows better than we do. He knows where you will fit perfectly.

The Perfect Roommate

At the end of my freshman year of college, I found myself without a roommate for the following year. It was somewhat of an awkward spot to be in. My current roommate was leaving the university, and all of my friends had already paired up for the following year. I had two options—let the university randomly assign me someone (which usually was not a good idea), or go to the housing office and pick a person myself out of the book of photos and housing applications. I chose the latter.

What no one really knew was that I was devastated by the whole thing. In a lot of ways I felt rejected and cast aside. I had one offer to room with a girl I knew, but we wouldn't have been compatible. So the entire way to the housing office I prayed that God would grant me favor and lead me to a great roommate. The only thing worse than not having a roommate for the next year would have been having a horrible roommate for the next year.

As I began flipping through the big binder of potential room-mates, and I scanned the lists of their habits and interests, I began to feel as if college life wasn't for me. It seemed like I wouldn't fit with anyone.

Finally, one girl's face jumped out at me from among the photos. She looked friendly and inviting. Her habits didn't seem too annoying. She was from out of state and would be a freshman the following year. So on a whim and a prayer I picked her, and she turned out to be the most easygoing of all of my roommates.

We had a great year. I began to see that it wasn't that I didn't fit at Biola; I just hadn't fit (roommate wise) with the girls I had already met. Through this roommate crisis, God graciously led this square peg (me) to a square hole, and things finally fit together nicely. Sometimes we just need to give God time to lead us to where He wants us to go.

I could have tried to convince the girls I knew that I would be the best roommate ever. I could have put on a mask and tried to make myself something I wasn't and live with the girl who wanted to be my roommate. But I knew faking compatibility was never going to work. If I had to live with someone for an entire year, I wanted the freedom to be myself.

JUST BE YOU

Howard Hendricks once said, "Great impressions can be made from a distance, but reality can only be tested up close."[1] A lot of times, when we try to be someone we're not, it will catch up with us. If we hang out with a group of athletes, and we want them to think we are athletic, it will only work until we are put in a situation where our athletic ability is tested. The same goes with being musically inclined or being a great artist.

My first job was as a receptionist at a children's gymnastics studio. The only other people who worked there were coaches. They were all extremely well built and athletic. In elementary school I took a dance class and in eighth grade I played softball, but wanting to impress my athletic friends, I made it sound like my athletic pursuits were a little more recent.

After a good six months of working there, some of them decided to go snowboarding, and they invited me along. Eager to fit in, I went. And I spent the entire day on my rear end on the bunny slope! By the end of our trip they definitely knew I did not have an athletic bone in my body.

You would be surprised at the number of girls I have met who have told me the same story. They boasted about how many guys they had kissed in an attempt to impress a certain group of people, when the truth was they had *never* been kissed and were too embarrassed to admit it. (On a side note, keeping yourself pure is something to *boast* about, not be embarrassed about.) As a result of their charade, all of a sudden they had the interest of many guys who wanted to take advantage of their so-called experience.

These girls wound up giving away their first kisses (and sometimes more) to guys who meant nothing to them in an attempt to gain popularity. Inevitably, all of them ended their story with the same regretful sentence: "I wish I just would have been me."

Learning to be *you* can be a tough thing for many reasons, but one seems to stand out above the rest. First, it can be extremely hard to be yourself when you have no idea who you really are. As you grow up, you are given a little freedom and your own identity apart from your family. Sometimes it is overwhelming and tough to determine what you believe and what you stand for—and why.

In order to conquer this problem, you need to discover who

you are—the person God made you to be. Psalm 100:3 says, "Know that the Lord Himself is God; it is He who has made us, and not we ourselves." And God didn't make us to just sit around here on earth and try to have a good time. He made us for a purpose. He made us to glorify himself. When He made you, He broke the mold. No one else on earth is exactly like you.

Unique and Individual Plans

I know seventeen-year-old identical twins, Hana and Sam. They look enough alike to be sisters, but with different hairstyles and their own style of clothing, you wouldn't necessarily know they are identical twins. Each of them embraces God's will for her life and what that entails. And even though they are *identical* twins, God's plans for them are completely different. Sam is a very gifted musician and worship leader, whereas Hana's gifting and passion is to work with children. No two people, even twins, will have the exact same calling in life.

Ultimately the purpose of all of our lives is to glorify God, but each of us is called to do that in a different way. In his bestselling book *The Purpose Driven Life*, Rick Warren talks about each of us having our own unique SHAPE: **S**piritual gifts, **H**eart, **A**bilities, **P**ersonality, and **E**xperience.[2]

If you are struggling with who you are and what you are here to do, I strongly suggest you take some time to think about some of the gifts and passions God has given you. They may be more than hobbies—they might be part of the reason God has placed you where He has. They might be part of His calling on your life.

Warren goes on to say, "You will be most effective when you use your spiritual gifts and abilities in the area of your heart's desire, and in a way that best expresses your personality and experience."[3] Discover and embrace your SHAPE and remember: You'll speed up your discovery a lot by taking your masks off. Just be you.

Think for a moment about your spiritual gifts. (Consult the spiritual gifts quiz in the appendix if you need help discovering yours.) Are you gifted at teaching or encouraging others? Do you have a flair for hospitality? Ask the Lord to show you what spiritual gifts He has given you for His glory.

What about your heart? What is something that squeezes your heart? What is the one thing you just can't help but do? Maybe you have a passion to see underprivileged kids succeed in school. If so, look for a way to get involved with an after-school tutoring program. Perhaps you want to see homeless people come to Christ and be clothed and filled with warm food. Then look for ways to volunteer at a shelter in your area. Pray and seek God on how that fits into His plan for your life.

What about your abilities? Can you sing, dance, or play a sport? How can you use those gifts to build into other people for God's glory? Consider offering free lessons to those younger than you. I know a guy who gave guitar lessons to people in his community—and the first song he taught all of them to play was "Jesus Loves Me." What a great witnessing opportunity.

Think about your personality—are you an introvert or an extrovert? This will probably determine whether God would have you be in an upfront position of service to Him (like the teacher of a discipleship group) or behind the scenes (like the girl who sets out all of the snacks for the fellowship time after discipleship is over).

Look back on your past experiences. Have you gone through something that will allow you to relate to others going through a hard time? I have met many girls who have been involved with counseling and support groups for girls with eating disorders because they were at one time caught in that trap too. What is your SHAPE, and how can you use it for God's glory?

Not Driven By Fear

Another reason it can be hard to take our masks off and become real is because it makes us vulnerable. As much as we want to be known and loved for who we are, we are afraid of our weaknesses and insecurities being exposed. We think, *If people know the real me, they won't like me!*

Recently I had a conversation with a fourteen-year-old girl who told me she was hanging with the wrong crowd at school and getting into some trouble simply because she did not want to be known as a goody-goody. To her, that would just be the end of the world. She would not say she was a Christian, or even act like one, because she didn't want to bear the lack of popularity that she thought would come with it.

Another girl I knew spent all of her time with friends and tried to be accepted wherever she could fit in. Whatever she did, she never wanted to go home or invite others to her home. She didn't want people to know how horrible her home life was, so she wore a mask and painted her home life as perfect while looking for love and acceptance in other places. This led her down a path of lying and deceit that eventually cost her more than her friends and popularity—she paid with her integrity as well.

What she did not realize was that her friends would have been sympathetic and understanding if she had come clean about her family in the first place. It was the sense of betrayal she created with her lies that drove her friends away, not the reality of how horrible her home life was.

No matter how many masks we wear and how hard we try to

please those around us, there will always be people who will reject us and cast us aside. It is just part of life. You can never please everyone. But you can please God. He has outlined His code of conduct for us in the Bible. But it does not stop at that. This isn't about having a list of rules to follow. Pleasing God means being yourself—being the girl He made you to be. He made *you* a leader.

As Christians, we are all called to be leaders and ambassadors for Him. First John 4:18 tells us that perfect love casts out fear. And God's love for us is perfect. He is never going to reject us or judge us by our abilities. He's the One who gave us those abilities, and He gave them to us for a purpose. Because of His perfect love for us, we need not ever fear rejection. It does not matter who else casts us aside, as long as God turns to us with arms wide open.

There's a Danish proverb that says, "What you are is God's gift to you; what you do with yourself is your gift to God."[4] Be the *you* God made you to be, and be yourself (SHAPE and all) to the best of your ability for His glory.

My friend Megan was a phenomenal high school athlete. She was named senior girl athlete of the year just before she graduated. During that same year she took the time to coach a junior high girls' basketball team. She wasn't just their coach—she was also their role model. These girls looked up to her and imitated her.

They genuinely got excited to see her each week. They wanted to be like her in more ways than one. She was the big sister many of them didn't have. Using basketball as a tool, Megan taught these girls about life. She is an excellent example of someone who used her SHAPE for God's glory.

Hiding Behind Denial

When I think of people who tried to hide behind masks—or prevented people from knowing who they really were—Peter always comes to my mind. He stands out to me as the perfect example of someone who walked with Jesus and experienced the power of God at work in and through his life, yet in a faltering moment he forgot about all of that. At a time when he feared for his own life, he chose to hide his faith rather than lead.

Matthew 26:69–75 tells a story most Christians know very well. When Jesus was brought before Caiaphas the high priest, just before His death, Peter followed Him there from a distance. As he stood outside the courtyard gate he was questioned by a servant girl: "You too were with Jesus the Galilean" (v. 69). In this moment, when leading could have made a huge difference and honesty could have been pivotal, Peter reached for a mask and portrayed himself as something he wasn't. "I do not know what you are talking about," (v. 70) he said, pretending not to be a friend of Jesus.

This happened again—twice. And immediately following the third denial of Christ, Luke 22:61 tells us Jesus turned and looked at Peter, and a rooster crowed, just as He had predicted. Peter's story presents a very startling reality to all of us. When we fail to stand up and lead for Jesus, we ultimately deny Him.

When we are more concerned with wearing masks that will make us pretty and popular, we diminish the work He did for us on the cross. When we live double lives—being one person at home and another at school—we mock the One who created us for a purpose.

And when we choose to reject who God has made us, and we pretend to be someone else instead, we are essentially telling God that He didn't do a good enough job and that we know better than He does. Romans 9:20–21 says that the thing created cannot say to its maker, "Why did you make me like this?" We do not have the right to question God's authority as to why He made us the way He made us and others another way.

MADE IN HIS IMAGE

Genesis 1:26 tells us we were made in the image of God. His desire for us is that we would wear our own beautiful faces instead of cheap and ugly masks. When we try to fit in with the world, we are distorting the image of God in our lives; we give an incorrect picture of God to those around us. If our friends know we are Christians who are willing to do whatever it takes to fit in, then they will assume that there is nothing different about our lives.

He wants us to lead others to Him—not lead them astray.

If we have God and we still act as if we need the approval of the world, those who already have the world's approval will automatically assume that they do not need God, since He does not seem to be enough for us. This is not the message we want to portray to the world around us. Yes, God desires for us to stand up and lead, but He wants us to lead others to Him—not lead them astray.

St. Augustine once said, "Preach all you can, and if you must, use words." Your life speaks louder than any words you will ever say. What are you saying with your life? If your life was the only Bible those around you ever read, would they have an accurate picture of the gospel? Or would they be left confused, like those surrounding Peter that night at Caiaphas's house?

An Open Invitation

Don't get me wrong. Costume parties can be fun. In seventh grade I was invited to a murder-mystery birthday party; I got to spend the entire evening masquerading as a wealthy pilot. But at the end of the night, I was glad to let my hair down and put my own clothes back on. As safe as you might feel pretending to be someone you are not, being yourself always feels better. You were made to be you. No one else was made to be you, and you were not made to be anyone else.

God has sent you the invitation of a lifetime. And it is not to a costume party. Instead, it's to a celebration in your honor. The invitation He has given you is to *your life*. You have one chance to embrace Him and embrace who He has made you to be. You have an entire lifetime to glorify God with your SHAPE. The only condition to accepting this invitation is that you have to take off your masks and leave them behind. The truth is, when God looks at you, He sees Jesus. But many times you try to cover up His beautiful image with less attractive ones. Imagine that—we think Jesus needs to be touched up with our makeup kit in order to make Him look better.

I knew a teacher when I was growing up who kept a sign up in her classroom that read, *What is right is not always popular, and what is popular is not always right.* There will come a time, perhaps many times, when you will be required to choose between the two. In that moment you will be asked to step up and lead in what is right, or you can choose to stand back and follow as you hide behind a mask.

Masks might give you temporary safety and security. But they will prevent you from being known and loved for who you really are, which is what you really want. It's your life—you can do what you want with it. In the end it is your choice, and your choice alone.

Life is not a costume party. Be authentic, be real, *be you*.

FOR FURTHER THOUGHT:

1. What are some masks you tend to hide behind in an attempt to be popular? (e.g., sports, academics, fashion, etc.)

2. Do you tend to hide behind masks because you don't know who you are or because you are afraid of being vulnerable? What can you do about this?

3. Make a list of some of the things that make up your SHAPE. Ask a friend or leader to help you if you get stuck.

4. How does wearing a mask prevent you from being a girl who leads?

5. Like Peter, how has denial been one of the masks you wear in regard to your relationship with Christ?

LEADERSHIP IN ACTION:

Identify one area in your life where you tend to hide behind a mask in a way that may be damaging both to you and the reputation of Christ. Make a conscious and daily effort to break that habit. Admit to someone you trust that you tend to wear a mask in this area, and ask that person to hold you accountable.

Refuse to wear a mask, even if not doing so makes you vulnerable. If you tend to hide behind an athletic accomplishment, have someone call you on it every time you mention your ability or status. If you tend to follow the crowd, have a good friend point it out to you every time you start to follow. Embrace your SHAPE, and just be you.

Notes

1. As quoted in Charles Swindoll, *Tale of the Tardy Ox Cart* (Nashville: Word Publishing, 1998), 42.

2. Rick Warren, *The Purpose Driven Life* (Grand Rapids: Zondervan, 2002), 236.

3. Ibid., 248.

4. Ibid., 249.

4

Christian Cuss Words and Other Cheap Compromises

One of the most memorable chapels I ever attended as a student at Biola University was taught by Pastor Francis Chan; it occurred during the first semester of my freshman year. To this day, I can still quote his main points almost verbatim. I have never been so convicted in my life.

That day Mr. Chan taught on the concept of watering down sin in order to make it acceptable. My friend Katie and I nervously shifted in our seats and our faces began to grow hot as he began to go down a list. The one thing on the list that convicted us the most was what he said about the words we choose to say.

"We all know that there is a list of words known as cuss words that as Christians, we are not to say," Mr. Chan began. "So we make up our own version of these words, and compare ourselves to the world. And since what *we* are saying is not as bad as what *they* are saying, we think we are okay." A few jaws dropped all through the gymnasium at this point. But what he said next sent the entire room into stunned silence.

"But do you know what?" he went on. "There is no difference in God's eyes between what you *are* saying and what you are *not* saying, since your new words have taken on the same meaning as the other words. Christians have their own version of cuss words and coarse gestures, and God knows full well what we mean when we say and do these things."

My friend Katie and I hung our heads at this point. We knew what he was talking about—we were guilty. The point that popped the most for me that day was simply this: As Christians, we compare ourselves to the world, and if we come out better than they do, cleaner than they do, then we deem ourselves okay.

We have no regard for holiness and no real desire to grow spiritually. By comparing ourselves to the world, we attempt to get as close to the line of compromise as we can without going too far. Instead, we should be comparing ourselves to God, in whose image we were made, to see how far we still need to go in terms of growth, purity, and spiritual maturity. Somewhere along the line we got it backward. And we are paying dearly for it in our spiritual lives.

One thing I am *not* going to do is give you a list of words you can and cannot say as a Christian. Giving you a list of rules wouldn't help. Rules don't change your heart, but convictions do. So as we travel the duration of this chapter together, I want you to think of your own compromises—your own words that you have selected to replace the world's version of profanity—and see how they measure up, not in light of this world, but in light of God's magnificent glory.

I'm pretty sure you know the type of words I am talking about. Anywhere the world interjects a cuss word, we interject our words instead. Most of the time our words are equally as crass, and sometimes they are just as vulgar. Many times we use words we don't even know the definition of, and we would be horrified if we knew what we were really saying. Christian cussing has become a relatively popular phenomenon among this generation.

Any girl who desires to lead is going to have to start with the words she chooses to say, because that is one of the first things people will notice about her. Just as it is with any language, if you speak it fluently and you speak it well, people will think you are from the place where that language originated. And when you change your language or your location, you still tend to speak with an accent.

WHERE ARE YOU FROM?

My girl friend Sam married a man from Brazil, and when the two of them came to visit my friends and me in California, we noticed that Sam's husband (naturally) had a thick accent. Everywhere we went with the two of them, people would ask where he was from. It was obvious from the way he spoke that he was not an American. I wonder if those who listen to us speak ever think it is obvious that we *aren't* Christians.

One of my roommates in college was from Germany, and she spoke with a slight accent. When her parents and brothers came to visit, their accents were even thicker and more noticeable. The funny part was that her mom was an American, yet she had the thickest accent of them all after living in Germany for so many years. When we surround ourselves with the language of this world—in the music we listen to, the movies we watch, and the friends we choose—we tend to pick it up quickly. Soon we're speaking the world's language with an unmistakable accent.

My husband's family is from New York, while I have lived in California my entire life. There are some words the two of us just pronounce differently. My husband's accent is not as noticeable as everyone else's in his family (on most words), since he moved to California when he was five. But when you gather his parents, grandparents, and aunts and uncles together, it is evident that they are your classic Italian family from New York. They speak with strong accents. At first, their accents sounded funny to me. But then they began to tease me about the way I said certain words. Oddly enough, they thought *I* was the one with the accent.

Many times new Christians carry a heavy accent. They bring

some of the profane terminology they used to freely use into their new life, where it seems out of place. It sends off warning bells to those around them, indicating that the new believers have not yet matured in their faith.

Of course, it will naturally take some time for them to weed out some of their old vocabulary and fully embrace their new life as a Christian. But there is something about Christians who cuss that reeks of immaturity or an insincere commitment to Christ. It may even lead some people to believe that they are double-faced hypocrites. As girls who aspire to lead, I know that is not our intention. So we need to be aware of this danger.

Cussing isn't the only thing that may confuse those around us or cause them to stumble. Saying we are Christians when we don't live like it can even be interpreted as taking the Lord's name in vain. Think about it for a minute. If you say you are a Christian and you represent Christ, but you live like someone who doesn't even acknowledge His existence, *you are making a mockery of Him.* You are making a very loud statement that Christ is not important to you on any level.

Exodus 20:7 says, "You shall not take the name of the Lord your God in vain, for the Lord will not hold him guiltless who takes His name in vain" (NKJV). Wow! That's a pretty harsh statement. I don't know about you, but I certainly don't want to stand before God and be found taking His name in vain.

The way we speak defines us. It helps people know where we are from and how we were raised. If we choose to use the world's terminology, and we use certain words or phrases that non-Christians use, the automatic assumption of everyone around us will be that we are not Christians.

I am not being a legalist here. The Bible is very clear on how we should speak. In Ephesians 4:29 it tells us, "Let no unwholesome word proceed from your mouth, but only such a word as is good for edification." This isn't just about avoiding profanity. We shouldn't let *anything* unwholesome come out of our mouths. And we should acknowledge our love and respect for Jesus Christ in how we speak.

WHAT'S IN A NAME?

Most people, sometimes even Christians, think that the words we use aren't that big of a deal. I beg to differ. You know why? As Christians, we are a reflection of Christ. We wear His name. Think about that for a second. We are *Christ*ians. Before I was married, my last name was Kubiak. It was the name I was born with, my family name. Because I bore that name, everything I did was a reflection on my parents. As a Kubiak, I represented them and our family unit. People would assume things about my parents by the way I behaved and interacted with others.

When I got married, my last name changed to Primicerio. All of the sudden my actions were a reflection on my husband and how we will choose to run our own family. People make assumptions about my husband based on what they know about me. Quite often, after I speak at an event, people will come up and ask me if my husband speaks at similar events for teenage boys. Most of the time they do not even know Michael's name or anything about him; they simply know me and know that he and I are one, and that is all they need to know in order to invite him out to their church.

In the same way, you and I are one with Christ. Jesus Christ no longer roams the earth in flesh and blood as He did in the past. We are the closest thing to Christ that people are going to *see* at this time in history. If we bear His name, people will make assumptions about Him based on our words and our actions.

That is a scary thought. If someone had to judge Christ's character based on overhearing one conversation you and your friends had at school, would they have a correct perception? *Depends on the conversation*, you might think. It shouldn't, because you never know who is listening and what your impact on them is.

Wearing Our Name Well

Several years ago I was flying to a writers' conference. I was seated next to a nineteen-year-old boy. I wasn't married yet, and I saw him check my finger for a ring before entering into a conversation. I could tell he was trying to impress me by the way he sat up straight and cleared his throat before speaking. He began the conversation by telling me how exhausted he was from the big party he had attended the night before.

He used several expletives and went into great detail about all of the drinking that went on at this party. When he saw he wasn't eliciting the response he desired, he shifted gears and asked me why I was on the flight. When I told him I was an author and was traveling to a conference, he asked me what kind of books I write. When I informed him that I wrote nonfiction books for Christian teen girls, he excitedly exclaimed, "Oh, I'm a Christian!" What I really wanted to say was, "Yeah, like I'm going to believe that." But instead I began to ask him about his background in the church, which was a conversation that dead-ended pretty quickly.

That young man may have been a Christian, but he most certainly was not wearing his name very well. What he said and how he chose to say it defined him. It didn't matter what title he chose to give himself. In my mind, his reputation had already been formed.

That is the way it works with all of us. Every time we speak, people form opinions about us. While we are not responsible for the opinions they form, we *are* responsible for the information we give them, out of which they form their opinions. And we must remember that they are not just forming opinions about us; they are forming opinions about Christ if we are publicly proclaiming ourselves as Christians.

If you are going to call yourself a Christian, then you'd better behave and speak like one, because you are a representation of Christ. If you don't want to imitate Him, then don't wear His name. There is no need for you to drag Christ's name through the mud with your bad lifestyle choices.

> *If you don't want to imitate Him, then don't wear His name.*

If you live one way and preach something else, you are messing with the reputation of an almighty God, and you are tampering with the souls of the unsaved people around you by giving them a distorted version of the gospel message. In God's eyes, that is no small offense. Galatians 6:7 tells us that God will not be mocked.

Deuteronomy 27:18 tells us we are cursed if we mislead a blind person on the road. If we are leading nonbelievers astray by the things we do and the things we say, we are not any better off than someone who leads a blind person into a ditch.

PICK IT UP

Those of us who take a public stand as a Christian do not realize how many people are watching us and how many will follow us simply because of who we say we are. There are those younger than you, or the same age as you, who are desperately searching for righteousness and truth. If you call yourself a Christian, they will want all your faith has to offer them—and they will imitate you as you supposedly imitate Christ.

A poem by Guy King perfectly illustrates this point:

I lost a very little word
Only the other day.
It was a very nasty word
I really had not meant to say.
But then, it was not really lost
As from my lips it flew,
My little brother picked it up
And now he says it too.[1]

Your friends, siblings, and sometimes people you don't even know will pick up the words you drop and begin to say them too. That is why it is so important that as Christians, we are wise in the words we choose to speak. It is easy to pick up words used by those close to us.

In high school my friend Jonathan had a bad habit of following every statement he made with, "You know what I'm saying?" Eventually all of us picked up this habit, and years later several of us still say it because it is now ingrained in us. Words are perhaps some of the easiest things we will ever pick up in our lives. Half of the time we adopt them without even realizing it. Imagine with me for a moment that what you were picking up was not words, but pieces of either gold or broken concrete instead.

Let's say you and your best friend are walking behind two people you know from school—one who is an outspoken authentic Christian and the other who claims to be a Christian but does not live like it at all. As you are walking behind these two girls, the first girl keeps dropping pieces of gold behind her as she walks. Every time she drops one, you effortlessly stoop down, pick it up, and put it in your purse. But the girl your best friend is walking behind is dropping large pieces of broken concrete behind her every few feet as she walks. Your best friend effortlessly bends down, picks up the pieces, and puts them in her purse every time one is dropped.

By the time you have walked a few miles, you would notice that you have a significant amount of wealth growing in your purse. For you the journey would be worth it, and you would want to keep going because it would be bettering your life. Your best friend, however, would be several steps behind you, unable to shoulder her heavy and pointless load without considerable effort. As you are being built up and invested in, your best friend would be getting weighed down and crushed under the weight of her load.

When we think of it this way, picking up foul language or cheap compromises doesn't seem as appealing, does it? I think many Christians speak freely without thinking because they do not understand who they really are or who they represent. Sure, we can get a handle on the fact that we are Christians. But we cannot seem to understand that we are royalty and grasp all that our position in Christ entails.

You Are a Princess

In the movie *The Princess Diaries*, Anne Hathaway plays Mia—a socially challenged fifteen-year-old girl—who finds out that she is really the princess of a small European country called Genovia. She knows nothing about being a princess and has no clue about how to be royal in any sense of the word. But her grandmother—the queen, portrayed by Julie Andrews—takes her through an intense training process in order to prepare Mia for a royal banquet at which she must appear.

This unfolds into a hysterical series of events involving hair straightening, makeup application, learning to walk in high heels, wearing contact lenses, and receiving a brand-new wardrobe. By the end of the movie, Mia looks like a brand-new person. She looks like royalty. But the irony is that *she has been royalty all along.* She just had to learn how to culture herself in order to accurately represent her kingdom. She remains true to herself and her personality, yet she still rises to the occasion of becoming ... well, royal.

> *There is a certain expectation that comes with being royal.*

You are a daughter of the King of Kings. When you tell someone you are a Christian, you are admitting your royal heritage. You do not necessarily have to say that you are a princess, but there is an underlying admission of that fact that other Christians will understand. And there is a certain expectation that comes with being royal.

Granted, we are adopted royalty (Romans 8:15), so sometimes royal behavior needs to be cultivated in us; it does not come naturally. Nevertheless, we are representatives of Christ and His kingdom. Just as we would not expect to travel to England and meet their queen with foul language and disrespectful behavior, in the same way people do not expect Christians to come to them and speak like that either. It somehow mars the reputation of not only that royal individual, but also the entire kingdom.

First Peter 2:17 tells us we should fear God and honor the king. This does not mean we should be afraid of God, but that we should honor and reverence Him as His holiness deserves. A big part of that means taking extra time and effort to make sure that we are accurately representing Him and His kingdom in the way we speak.

As His daughter, you are His representative to all of those around you. And for those who have never met the King themselves, you are their only connection to the royal family. Their entire view of God will be based on your behavior. Make a good impression on His behalf—He deserves it.

OUR WORDS REFLECT OUR HEARTS

Before we can ever effectively clean out our vocabularies, we must clean out our hearts. In Psalm 19:14 King David writes: "Let the words of my mouth and the meditation of my heart be acceptable in Your sight, O Lord, my rock and my Redeemer."

The things we choose to meditate on and set our hearts on have a direct impact on the words we will use. Luke 6:45 tells us, "Out of the abundance of the heart his mouth speaks" (NKJV). If our hearts and our minds are set on popularity, we will use the words that the popular people at school use. If our hearts and minds are set on winning the affections of a certain boy at school, it is more than likely that we will begin to use the vocabulary he and his friends use in an attempt to show him that we really are his kind of girl. If our hearts and minds are set on pleasing our friends, we will pick up the words they tend to drop as they go through their day.

But if our hearts are set on Christ, we will only use words that bring Him glory. It may take time, concentration, and effort to weed out some words and phrases we have become accustomed to using. But we will be willing to put that time and effort into it because we will have a true understanding that life is not about us; it's about God and His glory.

What are the words of your mouth and the meditations of your heart? Are they acceptable and pleasing in God's sight? Does your speech accurately reflect Christ's kingdom and your royal heritage to everyone with whom you come into contact?

Are you a girl who leads in the way you speak as well as in the way you act? Sure, actions may speak louder than words. But trust me, no matter how you act, people will not be able to see Christ in you if all they hear coming from your mouth is profanity. And I'm not just talking about the world's version of cuss words here. I'm talking about the watered-down Christian versions that we have so easily come to accept these days.

Hey, I'll be honest with you. I'm guilty of this at times too. I used to wonder who decided which words were bad and which words were good. Finally I realized that it doesn't matter who decided. The fact is that some words need to be off limits in a Christian's life if we are going to make a difference in this world for Christ. Anything else is a compromise, and compromise is a leader killer.

Stop comparing yourself to the world. Chances are, you will always look a little cleaner than you really are when you do that. When you hold yourself up to black, dirty white still looks white. It's when you compare yourself to pure white that you realize just how dirty you really are. Compare yourself to Christ—whose image you were made in—and see how far you still have to go. Then aspire to grow in that direction.

In college my friend Erin wrote me a note that revolutionized the way I saw myself and therefore revolutionized the way I spoke and behaved. Her note simply said:

> You are a child of the living God, the King of Kings and the Lord of Lords. You have the right to call the God of creation "Daddy." You have royal blood pumping through your veins. You are a princess in every sense of the word. As a child of the King, you have nothing to be ashamed of. Hold your head up high. Think like a princess. Speak like a princess. Act like a princess. Your Daddy is the King.

If we are ever going to accurately reflect Christ and His kingdom here on earth, we must do what Erin said and think like princesses, speak like princesses, and act like princesses. We cannot do just one of those things. If we are ever to be effective, we must do all three. Earlier in this book we talked a little bit about acting and thinking like a princess. It's time to go and speak like one as well.

FOR FURTHER THOUGHT:

1. Does your vocabulary tend to be an area where you struggle? Do you find yourself struggling more with actual cuss words or the watered-down Christian versions?

2. If people had to make a decision about Christ based on the words you use in conversations with friends, would they have an accurate reflection of who Christ is? Why or why not?

3. Do you find that you tend to measure yourself against the world's standards to see how good you come out? Or do you measure yourself against God's standards to see how far you have left to go? Why do you think that is?

4. What are the meditations of your heart at this moment, and how do they affect the words of your mouth?

5. How can viewing yourself like a princess help you more accurately reflect Christ in your speech?

LEADERSHIP IN ACTION:

Make an effort to only drop pieces of gold for others to pick up. Designate a certain day to make a conscious effort to do this. When you make a mistake or slip up and drop pieces of concrete instead, go and find a small stone and put it in your pocket or your purse. At the end of the day, count your stones in order to see how hard you need to work at this on a consistent basis.

Notes

1. As quoted in Charles Swindoll, *The Tale of the Tardy Ox Cart* (Nashville: Word Publishing, 1998), 531.

5

Coloring Inside the Lines

At the time I write this, my husband and I have thirteen nieces and nephews, with the fourteenth on the way—all from his side of the family, since I am an only child. More than half of them are currently under the age of five. When we visit them, they inevitably pull out their crayons and markers and begin to draw. Emma and Alyssa can be quite the artistic geniuses, but the boys usually hand us a scribbled mess of green and blue when they are done.

A scribbled mess is cute when it comes from a toddler who tries his hardest to make something to give you. It can be quite another thing when that scribbled mess is your life. Even those of us who are not into art can admit that we would rather have our lives come out looking like a neatly colored picture instead of the crayoned drawings that grace the refrigerators of my husband's siblings.

God is the master artist, yet so often we fight with Him over who should be holding the crayons. Psalm 100:3 says, "Know that the Lord Himself is God; it is He who has made us, and not we ourselves." That means you are God's masterpiece. He made you. He knows why He made you and in what conditions you will operate best. He knows what colors to splash on the canvas of your life. He has your best interest at heart, and He knows just where to draw guidelines and boundaries for you as you color in the details of your life.

If you stay within His lines, your life will be a beautiful masterpiece in the end. Notice I said *God's* boundary lines, not man's. Many times mankind gets confused over what it means to be made in the image of God; certain people begin to think they *are* God, laying down mandates and rules left and right. They think they are "junior God," as Beth Moore would say.[1]

When I was growing up, my family briefly attended a church where the pastor told my mom she could no longer teach the women's Bible study if she persisted in wearing knee-length skirts. She either had to wear ankle-length skirts or step out of her teaching ministry. Because there was nothing immodest or inappropriate about what she was doing, this is a perfect example of one of man's rules. In Christ, we are all still allowed the freedom to reflect our individual personalities and interests. God made us different from one another for a reason.

Although we need to have a healthy respect for those in authority, it's God's rules that are outlined in Scripture that we really need to work at following. It's God's boundary lines we need to stay inside of because He put them there for good reason, not because He was on a power trip. God's boundaries include things like loving God above all else, loving our neighbors as ourselves, not committing murder, adultery, and sexual immorality, honoring our parents, and not letting unwholesome words proceed out of our mouths. The boundaries God sets for us are unchanging principles that were established in biblical times and are still completely relevant today.

In their bestselling book *Boundaries*, Doctors Henry Cloud and John Townsend define boundaries as keeping good things in and bad things out.[2] It should seem pretty simple to remember, but all too often in everyday life we get so caught up in what is going on around us that we take everything in and leave nothing out. Girls who set firm boundaries in their lives and take heed to the commands God gives in the Bible will emerge as spiritual leaders.

BIBLICAL BOUNDARIES

There are many boundary lines drawn for us in the Bible. And they are all intended to help us let in the good things in life, the pleasures God himself created, and to keep out the bad things, the things that will be harmful and devastating to us. Let's look at just a few of those boundaries.

> Therefore do not let sin reign in your mortal body so that you obey its evil desires. Do not offer the parts of your body to sin, as instruments of wickedness, but rather offer yourselves to God, as those who have been brought from death to life; and offer the parts of your body to him as instruments of righteousness. (Romans 6:12–13 NIV)
>
> Therefore I urge you, brethren, by the mercies of God, to present your bodies a living and holy sacrifice, acceptable to God, which is your spiritual service of worship. And do not be conformed to this world, but be transformed by the renewing of your mind, so that you may prove what the will of God is, that which is good and acceptable and perfect. (Romans 12:1–2)
>
> Run in such a way that you may win. (1 Corinthians 9:24)
>
> Come back to your senses as you ought, and stop sinning. (1 Corinthians 15:34 NIV)
>
> Be on the alert, stand firm in the faith, act like [women], be strong. Let all that you do be done in love. (1 Corinthians 16:13–14)

Time after time, in book after book, the Bible tells us to flee sin and embrace God. It tells us to be firm in our faith and to be strong in our convictions. God tells us in His Word that sin is a very real thing and we are to avoid it at all costs. But sometimes sin can be fun and appealing. Sometimes the pressure to sin in order to fit in can be overwhelming. (We'll look at a few real-life examples in a minute.) When we ignore that reality, we begin to color outside of the lines, making our lives one huge scribbly mess. It is vitally important that we seek to lead others instead of being led astray, making a conscious effort to color inside the lines.

STAYING WITHIN THE LINES

As well intentioned as they are, some of my nieces and nephews do not know how to color within the lines. They see a crayon and they want to run with it, coloring their world. Sometimes it ends up on the walls, other times on the carpet, and many times on their clothes. And if I am around them and not paying attention, it will wind up on my clothes too. Crayons and markers can become dangerous things in the hands of toddlers. Freedom can become even more dangerous in the hands of teenagers.

Each of us reaches a place in our lives when we begin to taste independence: we turn thirteen and become teenagers; we turn sixteen and get our driver's license; we turn eighteen and become legalized adults. And with the enthusiasm of a toddler with crayons, we run around, trying to color our world. *Forget about rules and boundaries,* we think, *I've hit the big time now.*

We break curfews we think we don't need; we begin "going out" with boys when our parents tell us we are too young to date, and we drive faster than the speed limit allows. Sometimes we color outside of every single line we can find *just because we can.* By doing so, we display our immaturity and prove our need for guidelines and boundaries.

My sophomore year in college I lived in the dorms, and "Pamela" moved in next to me. One afternoon I was in my dorm room studying for a test when really loud rap music came blaring from Pamela's room. It was so loud it caused the wall between us to shake. One picture frame even came crashing down. Annoyed, to say the least, I went marching over to Pamela's room and pounded on her door with my fist. After several minutes of this, I realized that no one was even in the room. So I went to our Resident Assistant's room and asked her to open Pamela's door and turn off the music.

Just as we were unlocking her door, Pamela came flying down the hallway. In exasperation I turned to her and asked, "Why on earth would you turn your music up as loud as it can go, and then lock your door and leave?" She looked at me like *I* was the crazy one before answering.

"It's not quiet hours," she said, referring to our ten-o'clock noise curfew. "So I can do whatever I want with my music."

Having lost close to an hour of study time for my test, I looked at her and then at our Resident Assistant. I mumbled something about there needing to be rules against this and walked away in disbelief. Looking back, I wish I would have thought to quote 1 Corinthians 10:23 to Pamela: "All things are lawful, but not all things are profitable. All things are lawful, but not all things edify."

Her rationale didn't make any sense at all. But we all tend to use this kind of rationale when it is convenient for us. *It's my life*, we think, *I can do whatever I want.* But just because we *can* doesn't mean we *should*. It seems to me that few girls today draw a distinction between the two. Those who do, however, tend to emerge as leaders because they know when to say no.

> Just because we can doesn't mean we should.

Just as the lines in children's coloring books exist so that each page actually becomes a picture, drawing firm boundary lines between what we can do and what we should do will help us make a beautiful picture, not a big mess, out of our lives.

Just Say No

It usually takes only one little word to prevent a whole lot of pain. But something strange happens to us as we get older. We feel as if all we have heard for our entire lives is the word no. I'm sure if I asked you how many times your parents said no to your pleading requests, you would tell me there are too many times to count.

When we enter our teenage years, we gain a new sense of authority in our own lives. We begin to gain independence, and we don't think we need our parents' counsel and guidance as much as we did when we were younger. As we begin to make our own decisions, we are inclined to say yes to everything, embracing the world with open arms. It's like we want to make up for all the times we have heard the word *no* in our earlier years.

I saw a lot of this happening in college. I even experienced some of it myself. Many girls on my dorm floor changed dramatically within the first year of college. Many girls who arrived on campus without a stitch of makeup wound up coloring their hair and painting their faces more than the rest of us. Maybe they weren't allowed to wear makeup in high school, or perhaps they just chose not to wear it. I don't know the reasons for it happening. What I do know is that as they were given a little freedom, a little room to "find themselves," they often went wild in their responses. It didn't stop with makeup. Many girls changed their entire wardrobes, tastes in music and movies, and their study habits.

For those of us who lived with them, it was a gradual progression. But for their parents, who only saw them occasionally, it was a shock when they came to visit. I remember hearing many mothers say things to their daughters like, "Your hair, it's just so ... so ... different. Don't you like it longer?"

Changing your hair color and style, wearing more makeup, and even changing your tastes in fashion and movies are not necessarily bad things. In some ways, they are very natural changes we all go through as we grow up. They can actually be healthy ways to express freedom and independence, as long as we are not breaking any of our parents' rules. But there are many areas into which our free spirits wander that can put us on very dangerous ground. That's why it is important to know how and when to use the word *no*.

When I surveyed several high school girls and asked them what areas they struggled with most, they told me that their biggest battles had to do with the pressure to be thin (leading to eating disorders), cutting themselves, sexual pressures, and temptations to drink and smoke. Some of these girls had given in to the temptations. Others were fighting hard against them.

Some knew the power of the word *no* and used it often; others thought they would eventually get around to using it—if things got too out of hand—but they wanted to experience a little freedom first.

My friend "Alexis," who is a Christian and was even raised in Christian schools, gave that a try once. When her parents were out of town, she and her brother decided to have some friends over. They weren't planning a raging party, but they weren't sticking to innocent fun either. Even though several people there were underage, Alexis said nothing about the alcohol they brought. She even ended up drinking with them. Although she says she didn't drink a lot, she knew at the time that she should have said no. She gave in because she figured she wouldn't be driving anywhere afterward, so what harm could it do?

Later that night her boyfriend began to pressure her sexually, and she was so drunk she consented. It wasn't rape because she still had an idea of what she was doing. But when she woke up she felt awful, like she had been violated. She was ashamed and embarrassed, and had many regrets. Looking back, she realizes saying no to having a party while her parents were away, and saying no to the alcohol offered to her, would have prevented her from being in a situation where losing her virginity was an option. She is not the only one I know who wishes she would have used the word a little more often and a little more forcefully.

Several years ago I had lunch with a young woman who got pregnant when she was eighteen years old. She married the child's father but later found out that he had an affair with someone else before the baby was even born. This young mom came to Christ through the experience and has been walking with Him ever since.

Although she loves her baby and has forgiven her husband, her life didn't turn out the way she would have liked. She suffered a lot of unnecessary pain and heartache because she didn't know how to say no. Looking back, she wishes she would have been wiser. Thoughts of fleeing immorality and not letting sin reign in our mortal bodies should be running through all of our minds constantly. We cannot let our guards down, not even for a second.

Wanting to experience freedom was not the only reason these girls chose to "color outside the lines." They also felt a tremendous amount of pressure from those around them. I do not think any of us realize the impact we have on our peers, and the impact they have on us.

Everybody's Doing It

In his book *Hide or Seek*, Dr. James Dobson tells the following story:

A few years ago psychologist Ruth W. Berenda and her associates carried out an interesting experiment with teenagers designed to show how a person handled group pressure. The plan was simple. They brought groups of ten adolescents into a room for a test. Subsequently each group of ten was instructed to raise their hands when the teacher pointed to the longest line on three separate charts. What one person in the group did not know was that nine of the others in the room had been instructed ahead of time to vote for the second longest line.

Regardless of the instructions they heard, once they were all together in the group, the nine were not to vote for the longest line, but rather vote for the next-to-longest line.

The desire of the psychologists was to determine how one person reacted when completely surrounded by a large number of people who obviously stood against what was true.

The experiment began with nine teenagers voting for the wrong line. The stooge would typically glance around, frown in confusion, and slip his hand up with the group. The instructions were repeated and the next card was raised. Time after time, the self-conscious stooge would sit there saying a short line is longer than a long line, simply because he lacked the courage to challenge the group. This remarkable conformity occurred in about seventy-five percent of the cases, and was true of small children and high school students alike.[3]

How many times have *you* done something simply because you did not want to be left standing alone? Recently I spoke with a girl who gave in to sexual pressures because she was at a party where a lot of people were getting physical. She admitted she didn't really want to do it, but she didn't want to be the only one who said no.

After a little prodding, she also admitted that she had been able to refuse the unwanted advances of another guy when she was alone. It was somehow easier to say no when her friends weren't around.

Now, I am not saying it is a good idea to be alone with a guy, because it is just as easy (and for some, easier) to give in to sexual temptation in that situation. But for this particular girl, the peer pressure was so intense that she didn't even consider how she was compromising her purity until after the fact.

LIVING WITH PURPOSE

One of the best things you can do for yourself in regard to coloring within the lines, living within God's boundaries, is to simply make a list of things you will not compromise. For me, drinking, drugs, and sexual exploration were always off limits. So I made sure that I never allowed myself to be in a setting (like a Friday night party or at a certain friend's house) where these activities were taking place.

A friend of mine realized she could have a tendency toward an eating disorder, so she made a deal with herself: She could only work out if she ate, and she had to work out in proportion to what she was eating (no excessive workouts or meals made of only lettuce). *Map out your plan of action* because it is always easier to say no *before* you find yourself in a compromising situation than it is in the midst of it.

Before I was married, I got asked out by several unsaved guys from work or school. By simply saying no to these dates, I never found myself having to refuse their sexual advances. I also never accepted an invitation to a typical high school party. By declining the party invitation, I never had to say no to the drugs and alcohol there. By saying no when it was easy, I never had to say it when it was hard.

Perhaps some of the things you know you need to say no to don't seem like that big of a deal. Having to give them up may seem unfair to you. Maybe you think you will miss out on some fun. In times when life doesn't seem fair and you are feeling bummed out because you gave up something you really wanted out of obedience to God, try praying instead of sulking. Pray for those you know who are caught up in sinful lifestyles, knowing that they may face heavy consequences for the "fun." Don't envy them, because you have chosen a better alternative for your life-long term. Set an example—a cheerful and happy example—of what a life surrendered to the Lord looks like in an average teen-age girl. The impact you make by making the right choice in the simple everyday decisions in life may be a lot larger than you think.

People don't follow a crowd. Rather, they become part of a crowd that is following one person. Be that person. We live in a world that tells us "the majority rules." But as the historian Arnold Toynbee once said, "It is doubtful the majority has ever been right."[4]

People don't follow a crowd.

Do not be afraid to be different. Live with purpose, and decide in your heart that you will not defile yourself with the things that tempt others. Often, they are blind to what you see—the negative consequences of their behavior.

Sure, at times you may experience a little ridicule. But you'll be making God proud. He always prospers those who choose to honor Him with their choices. I have known many girls who lived with integrity on public school campuses and have received numerous honors, awards, and leadership positions *because* they were different and unafraid to stand out from the crowd.

Dr. James Dobson tells a compelling story about a blind teenager who refused to use a walking stick, and a deaf boy who refused to wear a hearing aid. Why? Well, it seems they would rather be blind and deaf than be different![5] We often treat our Christianity in much the same manner. We would rather compromise our faith than be different from the world. The saddest thing about that mentality is that those of us who know right from wrong will be even more grieved by the consequences of our actions. One day we will wake up like Alexis, wishing we would have said no back when it was easy to do so.

A Page is Turned

No matter what kind of decisions you have made in the past and how colorful the messes are that you have made up to this point, God is offering you a brand-new page in the coloring book of your life. He has drawn a picture of what He desires your life to be. It's up to you to add the color with your own personality and your own sense of flare. If you stay within the lines, you will have a masterpiece when you are through. But if you choose to scribble all over everything just because you can, the original picture will never be seen and all beauty will be lost.

God doesn't draw pictures of followers. He draws pictures of leaders. All Christians are called to be leaders in some capacity. All of us, for instance, are called to be leaders in how we live our lives. Lamentations 3:22–23 tells us that God's mercies are new every morning. That means every day you get a fresh start.

Like a loving father, God will clean your crayon marks off the walls and He will clean up the mess you have made of your life. He will hand you a fresh coloring page with a beautiful drawing of what He wants you to be, and He'll give you the most beautiful crayons in the entire box.

So go ahead. Color your world and make it beautiful. Use the brightest and most brilliant colors you can find. But please, whatever you do, *stay within the lines.*

FOR FURTHER THOUGHT:

1. Describe a time in your life when you felt like a toddler, running with crayons and trying to color your world. What did you do? What were the consequences? How did you feel afterward?

2. Look up verses that help explain what God's picture for your life might contain. List three. (Hint: Check out Jeremiah 29:11, Ephesians 3:20, and Romans 8:28 if you get stuck.)

3. Do you tend to seek freedom or acceptance? What are your specific weak areas? (Examples: boys, clothes, partying, etc.)

4. What have you purposed in your heart not to do? How do you plan to hold fast to those things in the midst of temptation?

5. Explain why it is important for a leader to be different than the crowd. How effective would her leadership be if she gave in to the crowd's wishes time after time?

LEADERSHIP IN ACTION:

Define an area in which it is hard for you to say no, then purpose in your heart that you will learn to exercise your right to say no to it. If you have friends who are pressuring you to drink or smoke with them, decide to make it easier on yourself; stop hanging out with them.

If you have a guy regularly calling you who is not a godly young man, refuse to talk to him. Politely tell him that you cannot talk and then hang up the phone. After a few times, he should get the hint. Be a leader this week. Say no to the things of this world, and live within the lines God has set for you.

Notes

1. Beth Moore, *The Patriarchs* (Nashville: LifeWay, 2005).
2. Henry Cloud and John Townsend, *Boundaries* (Grand Rapids: Zondervan, 1992), 31.
3. James Dobson, *Hide or Seek* as quoted in Charles Swindoll's *The Tale of the Tardy Ox Cart* (Nashville: Word Publishing, 1998), 434.
4. As quoted in Charles Swindoll's *The Tale of the Tardy Ox Cart* (Nashville: Word Publishing, 1998), 435.
5. Ibid., 433–34.

6

Guarding Your Heart

My friend "Carly" came to me recently and asked me to help her guard her heart. She was involved in a friendship that was blossoming into a deeper relationship just before her senior year of high school was to end. The guy, "Jeff," told her they should just be friends at this time in their lives, but his actions did not line up with his words.

He called her frequently. They went out to dinner together alone—and he paid for it. They hung out at each other's houses, just the two of them, frequently. In Carly's words, her heart had "already run ahead of her" in this friendship. She wanted my advice on how to catch up with it and slow it down.

"I know it's already too late. I am going to get hurt in some way," she said to me wistfully, "and that makes me sad." My heart broke for Carly because she was sitting in the very same place I had been sitting only a few years earlier. So I told her what I desperately wish someone would have told me. Not only did I tell her to guard her heart, like I had been told years before. I actually told her what that meant—which was something no one could answer for me when I was her age. Pain and experience had taught me the answer.

But before we begin our exploration of this topic, I want to briefly touch on a controversy that I find both unnecessary and highly destructive in Christian circles today—that is the debate over *dating* versus *courting*. You can engage in both of those activities without guarding your heart, and you can also guard your heart in both of those forms of relationship. The problem isn't with the method or what we call it; the problem is in how our hearts respond to the situation.

Any girl who desires to guard her heart and be a girl who leads will not be hung up on methods but will be committed to the truth. When it comes time for you to engage in a romantic relationship, it is important that you seek the Lord and talk openly with your parents as you reach the decision about what is right for you. I have seen blessings and devastation result from *both* dating and courting. And I even know of several girls (myself included) who have been deeply wounded by a *friendship* with a guy when the attraction was not mutual.

In his book *Boy Meets Girl*, Joshua Harris says:

> None of us should allow a debate over words to distract us from what really matters in relationships. "Dating versus courtship" isn't the point. I've known "serial courters" who lived like the devil and "saintly daters" guided by integrity and holiness. In and of themselves, the terms they used to describe their relationships were meaningless. The way they lived is what really mattered. Terms don't define our lives; our lives define our terms.[1]

The truth is, we need to guard our hearts in all of our relationships. Any time we open our hearts to someone else, we create the potential to be hurt. Guarding our hearts is not a one-time thing. It is something we need to do daily and in every relationship.

Guarding our hearts isn't just a principle; it is a practice. In friendship, dating, and courtship we open our hearts up and make ourselves vulnerable to other people—to other sinful and imperfect people. In her Bible study *Living Beyond Yourself*, Beth Moore says, "Rejection can happen anywhere relationship happens."[2] That is a scary thing. People *will* hurt us. People *will* let us down. Our hearts *will* be broken sometime in our lives. There is no maybe there. That is why guarding our hearts is so necessary.

Proverbs 4:23 tells us: "Above all else, guard your heart, for it is the wellspring of life" (NIV). What is a wellspring? *Dictionary.com* tells us it is "an abundant source." Our hearts are an abundant source of life. Why? Our hearts are where we connect with God. Haven't you ever heard of the phrase "Asking Jesus into your heart"? In John 10:10 Jesus says He came to bring abundant life to us. So if Jesus is residing in our hearts, you can bet our hearts are an abundant source of life.

But when we do not guard our hearts and do not protect that source of abundant life within us, we get trampled on and beaten up. Our wellsprings get clogged and no longer function like they should. And we wind up with a broken heart—a wellspring that doesn't work. I have been there many times, and I am sure you have been there once or twice too.

ON GUARD

When I was in high school I had a very good friend; we'll call him "Pete." He and I were the spiritual leaders in our group of friends. We both taught Bible studies and were the ones others came to for godly counsel. For a time there was a mutual attraction between us. I met Pete at the beginning of my sophomore year of high school, and it was the end of my junior year before I realized that things were not going to work out for us romantically.

During the time that the attraction was mutual, Pete called and came by often. We attended a school dance together; we prayed together and had many long talks about deep and spiritual things. He even made comments about what a godly wife I was going to make and how God was preparing him to be a godly husband, which sent my seventeen-year-old mind into wedding planning mode and naming our children. Shortly after that, he took another girl to my prom and broke my heart into a million pieces.

The pain was devastating. It took me a good two years to get over the rejection I felt, although it only took me a few months to get over Pete himself. About six months or so after Pete's rejection, another guy friend came into my life. We'll call him "Ben." He fell head over heels in love with me and treated me like a princess. I loved the attention of course, but the problem was that I didn't have the same feelings for Ben that he had for me. And instead of being open and up-front about that, I turned into a Pete in his life.

Ben and I would have long and deep conversations on the phone. We hung out together all the time. We went to a school dance together. I was the first person he called when he got off of work during the summer after our senior year. When I left for college, I broke his heart into a million pieces. At that point I was still too selfish to realize what I had done. The following summer, after I had my heart broken again, I called Ben in tears and apologized for the pain I had caused him.

With scars on my heart from my experiences with both Pete and Ben, I sat across the table at Starbucks with my friend Carly, who was seeking answers. I looked her square in the eye and explained to her how she could still protect both her own heart and Jeff's in this situation.

"You have two options," I told her. "You two either need to make a commitment to each other and take this to the next level, or you need to take ten steps back. That means no talking on the phone and no hanging out alone together. Any time spent together should be in large groups where you can't be singled out by him."

Carly nodded slowly. She did not like what I had to say, but she knew it was the truth.

Because Jeff had already admitted that he had feelings for Carly on an earlier occasion and had taken her out several times (and only because he had already done that), I encouraged Carly to write him a letter, explaining how her heart had run ahead of her and how they needed to make a choice, because what they were doing was destructive. Neither of them was being wise and taking steps to guard their hearts. Later that day she wrote a letter, asked me to proofread it, and dropped it by Jeff's house. She told him not to respond until he was sure of his answer.

Let Him Make the First Move

The advice I gave to Carly is *not* advice I would give to a girl who has feelings for a guy friend and is uncertain about how he feels about her. The girl should not pursue the guy. It almost never works when things develop that way. If a guy has not *told you* (with words, not just actions) that he likes you, do not assume he does. It's just safer that way. As girls, we have a tendency to read into things, and sometimes we think guys are sending signals when they are just being nice. Wait for a guy to verbalize his intentions to you before you ever let him know you are interested.

Then how will he know it is safe to pursue me? You probably have a million questions racing through your mind right about now. My response to this question is simple: Let God tell him. I know it works because it worked for me and so many others. I think it is a pretty sound (and safe) method.

In Matthew chapter one, the Scriptures tell us that God appeared to Joseph in a dream and told him to marry Mary. If you are somewhat of a blabbermouth like I am, and you have to talk to someone about your crush, talk to God about it first. Then, if you have a trusted youth leader or friend who can help you keep your head on your shoulders in all of the excitement that may ensue, by all means talk it over with her. But be careful about who you pick to talk to—it needs to be someone who will give you a godly perspective, not another girl friend who will simply encourage you in all your romantic notions.

For a girl who has not been told that she is liked by the guy of her dreams, writing a letter like the one I told Carly to write would *not* be guarding her heart. But for Carly it was, because feelings had already been verbalized yet no action was being taken, and it left her in the middle of a confusing mess. She needed clarification on what they were going to do about this mutual attraction, because lying to everyone about just being friends was not cutting it.

THE NUMBER ONE RULE

The number one rule about guarding your heart is being honest about your feelings and expecting (even demanding) that same level of honesty in return. Now, I do not say the word *demanding*, meaning stomping your feet and making a scene like a spoiled child in the toy aisle of Target. I simply mean choosing not to waste your time with guys who will not be honest and up-front with you. I encouraged Carly to give Jeff a chance to be honest with her, and if he could not come to a decision, she needed to pack up her heart and take it elsewhere, because he was definitely not worth her time.

After my experiences with Pete and Ben, I asked the Lord to bring me a guy who would be so direct and bold in his pursuit of me that it had to be God. In college, one poor guy sent me an e-mail professing his undying love for me. Unfortunately, the feelings were not mutual. So I sent him a kind reply, thanking him for his flattering remarks and compliments, but explaining that the feelings were not mutual. I went on to tell him that I did value him as a friend. I didn't want either of us to have any more Ben or Pete experiences. So I laid it all out on the table and was honest. This guy respected that, and we remained friends until he graduated and moved away. I guarded his heart, and things worked out just fine.

When my husband took me out on our first date, I was shocked and highly impressed with how up-front he was with me. He had even gone to my mom (since he did not know my dad) before taking me out to ask her if she had any reservations about it. On our first date, he made his intentions perfectly clear. We prayed about our relationship for a short time, and we have been together ever since.

There was no game playing, no second-guessing. I never once had to wonder how Michael felt about me because he always made his intentions clear. That is God's design for relationships. Game playing kills honesty and breaks trust before it is ever established. When you are open and up-front in the beginning, and the guy you are interested in is open and up-front with you, many problems will be solved before they start. But you need to make sure the guy makes the first move. Jeff was open in his interest toward Carly. But he was unclear in expressing the intention of that interest. That is why it was okay for her to initiate clarification about their relationship. Some people call this having a D-T-R: Define the Relationship Talk.

GIVING YOUR HEART AWAY TOO SOON

In high school I had two friends who received promise rings from boyfriends. One couple had dated for three years and the other had dated for four years. Both relationships ended in devastating breakups. Unfortunately, there is an increasing trend among teens to use the "m word," something that should not even be in any teen's vocabulary. Marriage should not be on the forefront of your mind when you are in high school. You're not ready to get married (no matter how mature you are), so why waste your time talking about it? Now, granted, I do believe you should only enter into a relationship with someone you think you could *potentially* marry. But letting some guy put a ring on your finger at fifteen is premature.

One of my two "pre-engaged" friends eventually decided that her boyfriend was not the right one for her and saw how settling too soon on her choice of a life mate meant she didn't have the option to figure out who else could be out there. Fortunately, she got out of the relationship before following through at the altar. She is now happily married to a solid Christian man. Her exboyfriend has since walked away from the Lord and is now married to someone else.

My other friend with a promise ring was in a relationship where they both realized they had settled too quickly and wanted to explore other options in life. Her boyfriend made a commitment to her that he just could not keep. He was not anywhere near ready to settle down. He gave her the ring simply because that is "what Christian kids do." Four years later they endured a devastating breakup.

She describes the relationship this way:

> I dated [Steven] for four years, and it was toward the end of the relationship that I felt like I was compromising on what God had for me in a life partner. It was the fear of losing him and being alone that tightened my grip. In my

heart I knew that [Steven] wasn't ready to get married, but I thought I could change that. Looking back on the situation I realize that I held on to [Steven's] promise, but I really didn't ask God if that was the promise He had for me.

Now, four years later, she is happily headed to the altar with a solid Christian man, while her ex-boyfriend is still out there trying to figure things out, not ready to settle down yet. She admits she could have saved herself from a lot of heartache had she not rushed into such a big commitment so young.

Their experiences teach us the importance of not giving our hearts away too soon. You should never, ever talk about marriage with a guy unless you are in a position to head to the altar in a year or less. You don't have to get married in a year or less, but if you are not in a position to do so, talking marriage is premature. At this point it is all talk, and many times it remains that—all talk. That can be a painful thing if you've banked your entire future on that talk. If the Lord leads you, entering a relationship that *could* result in marriage is an okay thing to do. But if you jump into a relationship and begin picking your bridesmaids right away, you are not guarding your heart, and the results can be devastating.

I'm not saying that nobody meets their future husband at fifteen. I'm simply saying that most people don't. Even if you do meet him at that age, you are still not ready to be a wife at fifteen. So don't prematurely step into that role by giving your heart away too fast. Make your prospective partner earn your trust and win your heart. Make him impress you; if he doesn't do this in the beginning, chances are he never will.

Do not give your heart away to a guy who is not in a position to care for you—spiritually, emotionally, and financially. If you are not engaged, do not allow yourself to talk with him about a wedding, marriage, or babies. To do so may cause far more harm than good. When Pete told me that God was preparing him to be a godly husband, my heart got wrapped up in a future that was not meant to be. Part of the reason I had such a hard time letting go after he had moved on to someone else was because in my mind, things were set in stone when in fact they never really existed at all.

Other Dangers to Avoid

It is also important to note other ways that girls tend to rush in relationships. An obvious one is physical contact—hugging, kissing, and holding hands. We'll talk more about that in another chapter. But one other important thing to note about guarding your heart is the level of spiritual bonding that occurs between a guy and a girl when they are not married or engaged. Reading your Bible, praying, and doing devotions are all good things to do. And you should look for a guy who does all of those things on a regular basis. But the two of you should continue to do these things *separately* until you move into another level of your relationship (engagement).

The reason may not be obvious at first glance. What we need to understand is that spiritual intimacy is just like physical intimacy; every time you create that bond with someone, you give a piece of yourself to him. Girls who bond spiritually with guys feel just as violated after a breakup as does a girl who has given herself away physically. One chapel speaker I had in college even coined the term "spiritual rape" to describe cases where guys attempt to bond spiritually with a girl because they think that is what they are *supposed* to do, and then they end up breaking up and taking off because they cannot handle that level of commitment.

One youth pastor I spoke with described it to me like this: "Being the spiritual leader in a relationship is the role of a husband—not the role of a boyfriend. We need to focus on teaching junior-high and high-school boys how to be men before we teach them how to be husbands. One naturally comes before the other."

I wholeheartedly agree with that statement. Yes, you should look for someone who will be a good spiritual leader. But make him prove that he is a man—in how he refuses to take things (both spiritually and physically) that are not yet his—before you let him sweep you off your feet. Jumping into a relationship and intensifying a spiritual connection just because you cannot go very far with your physical connection is *not* guarding your heart. This is why so many girls wind up hurt without even realizing what happened.

And if you create a tight-knit spiritual and emotional bond, it is only natural that you will feel the need to intensify your physical connection to balance things out. Spiritual closeness is dangerous ground for couples who are not married or engaged to be married. Make a guy earn your heart, and make him prove that he is worthy of your affections.

A Shining Example

A young couple I know, "Jacquelyn" and "Esteban," began courting when she was just fifteen. What she didn't know was that Esteban had gone to her parents when she was fourteen and asked them if he could pursue her. They told him to pray about it and come back in a year. So he did. In the beginning they allowed the two of them to hang out in well-supervised situations. Little by little, as they got older, they were granted a little more freedom. Then, when Jacquelyn was twenty, the two of them were finally married.

She describes their courtship like this:

One of the things I always admired about Esteban was how he guarded my heart in the year and a half he waited to tell me he liked me. I had no clue he had feelings for me. He always treated me like a friend and sister in Christ, unlike other guys who flirt and act like they like you and a week later decide they really don't.

Guys like that should be applauded.

For Jacquelyn and Esteban, guarding their hearts was easier because their romance slowly unfolded over time, and there was a lot of parental involvement that helped them in areas they were still too immature to understand. Also, Esteban treated Jacquelyn in a way that hid his romantic feelings until his intentions could be made known. Guys like that should be applauded. They know what guarding a girl's heart is all about.

It is also important to note that courting was Esteban's idea—he initiated it. Too many girls use courtship as a tool to draw some poor unsuspecting guy into a commitment he never intended to make. Just because you do something under the umbrella of a "solid" commitment like courtship does not mean you will be spared heartache. The type of commitment you make is not what makes something right or wrong for you; it's determined by the person to whom you are committing yourself.

BREAKING UP IS HARD TO DO

Before he ever met me, my husband courted another girl. It was the way her family did things, the way his friends did things, and it seemed like the Christian thing to do. He entered this relationship based on his emotions rather than on seeking God's will. And the results of this courtship were anything but God honoring. It almost severed his relationship with his parents altogether and created a lot of pain for many people on both sides of the relationship.

They had taken a seemingly good principle—courting instead of dating, so that they would not carry unnecessary baggage with them through life—and manipulated it to be what they wanted it to be. They just wanted to find someone to marry; they somehow missed the fact that God had a specific someone for each of them to marry, and it wasn't each other. Michael followed all of the right steps as to how to engage in a courtship and commit himself to this girl—but she was the wrong one for him. So God had to intervene and make things painful and uncomfortable enough that he would want out of the relationship.

Oddly enough, at this time I was away at college and had no clue who I would someday marry. But God put it on my heart for a period of several months to pray for my future husband, specifically asking God to show him that whoever he was with at the moment was not the one God had for him. I didn't even know Michael yet, and knew nothing about the relationship he was already in, but the Holy Spirit did. Years later, while looking through old journals from that time, I discovered that the Lord had me praying those prayers at the same time Michael was courting this other girl.

The lesson in this is threefold.

- First, do not commit yourself to a principle or course of action just because it seems like the right thing to do. Prayerfully seek the Lord on how and when to enter a relationship—and with whom—before you make any decisions. Before you accept the affections of a guy who is pursuing you, make sure he is the guy with whom God wants you to be involved. Spare yourself the baggage that broken relationships bring.

- Second, do not be afraid to get out of a relationship, no matter how serious it has become, if you feel the Lord is showing you it is wrong. You will spare yourself a lot of heartache, and the right guy just might be out there somewhere, praying that you will break up with this person who is wrong for you.

- The third lesson this story teaches us is to never underestimate the power of prayer. Pray for your future husband. You do not have to pray for him by name. But pray specifically. Ask the Lord to be building the character traits of a godly man in him. Ask the Lord to keep him pure for you. Ask the Lord to protect him from being drawn into relationships that are not of the Lord. And then pray—and live out—those very same things in your own life.

YOU ARE THE GIRL—NOT THE GUY

Many girls today cheat themselves—and go against God's design—when they make themselves the pursuers rather than the pursued. A lot of girls come to me and say, "It's not a big deal. It doesn't matter who does the pursuing, does it?" I beg to differ. It is a big deal. How do I know? God made Adam first. You might think that was mere coincidence, but I consider it to be part of God's divine design. Elisabeth Elliot says it best in her book *Let Me Be a Woman*:

> You can't make proper use of a thing unless you know what it was made for, whether it is a safety pin or a sail boat. To me it is a wonderful thing to be a woman under God— to know, first of all that we were *made* ("So God created man in His own image, in the image of God He created him; male and female He created them.") and then that we were made

for something. ("The rib which the Lord God had taken from the man he made into a woman and brought her to the man.")

This was the original idea. This is what woman was for. The New Testament refers back clearly and strongly for this purpose: "For man was not made from woman, but woman from man. Neither was man created for woman, but woman for man." Some texts are susceptible of differing interpretations, but for the life of me I can't see any ambiguities in this one.[3]

Woman was made for man. God brought Eve to Adam. He did not set her loose in the garden and tell her to go hunt down a man. Yet often that is how we live. We set our sights on some poor unsuspecting guy and put all of our effort into making him think we are the one God has for him. Whether we are or we aren't is not the point. The point is God brought Eve to Adam, and oddly enough Adam knew what to do from there. There was not even anyone around to tell him what to do other than God himself. God will show the Adam He has for you how to go about pursuing you when the time comes. Will you trust Him? It worked for Eve, and it worked for me. And it has worked for millions of other women throughout the ages.

Enjoy Your Singleness

One of the things that breaks my heart the most is seeing girls living for the affections of the guys in their lives. One of the biggest parts of guarding your heart comes from realizing that God did not make you half of a person. You are not incomplete when you are single. In Christ you are complete. In

You are not incomplete when you are single.

Christ you are perfect just as you are. In Christ you lack nothing. Right now, while you are single, you have even more of a potential to do incredible things for the Lord.

First Corinthians 7:32–34 says:

> I would like you to be free from concern. An unmarried man is concerned about the Lord's affairs—how he can please the Lord. But a married man is concerned about the affairs of this world—how he can please his wife—and his interests are divided. An unmarried woman or virgin is concerned about the Lord's affairs: Her aim is to be devoted to the Lord in both body and spirit. But a married woman is concerned about the affairs of this world—how she can please her husband. (NIV)

Now, I am (obviously) not telling you to never get married. What I am telling you to do is this: Enjoy your time of singleness, because it will not last forever. My single years were filled with mission trips, writing books, and speaking engagements. I could go wherever God asked me to go without holding back.

Now that I am married it changes things for me. I cannot accept every speaking invitation I receive, otherwise I would be gone almost every weekend of the year and would never see my husband. I'm a little more restricted when it comes to how and when I can minister now because I need to spend time with my husband and nurture our relationship as well.

Your day will most likely come. Unless you are called to celibacy—which truly is a calling—you will one day be a wife. At that time your unrestricted ministry opportunities will come to a close. Don't look back on these years—and specifically this year that you are in now—with regrets. Please don't have divided interests because of a certain guy. Don't pine away, hoping for a date with Romeo.

Focus on the Lord. Step up and be a girl who leads in how you interact with the guys in your life. Don't lead them on, chase them down, or let them play games with your heart. *Encourage them to be godly young men by being a godly young woman.*

Remember, as Beth Moore says, "The only environment needed for rejection is relationship."[4] So guard your heart and be wise.

FOR FURTHER THOUGHT:

1. Do you have any guy friends you have crushes on? Are you being honest with yourself about your feelings and your motives for being his friend? Are you guarding your heart? How so?

2. Have you had experience with not guarding your heart in the past? What happened as a result?

3. Are you more concerned with whether or not a guy would prefer to date or court than you are with who he is as a person? Would you be willing to enter into a relationship with someone who desired to use different terminology than you do? Why or why not?

4. At this place in your life, are you ready to be married? If not, how far should you let yourself go in relationships with the opposite sex (relationally, not physically)?

5. What are some practical ways you can guard your heart, considering your current circumstances and relationships?

LEADERSHIP IN ACTION:

Examine your friendships with the guys in your life. If you have been leading someone on, end it. Be gentle and kind in your approach. Make sure you let him know how much you value him as a friend, but make it *very clear* (with words and not just actions) that you only desire to remain friends.

If you fear that you are the one being led on, take several steps back from the relationship and distance yourself emotionally. If you have already communicated romantic feelings but have not stated your intentions for the relationship, then—like Carly and Jeff—pray about writing a letter and getting things out in the open. Whatever you do, guard your heart!

Notes

1. Joshua Harris, *Boy Meets Girl* (Sisters: Multnomah, 2000), 32.
2. Beth Moore, *Living Beyond Yourself* (Nashville: Lifeway, 1998), 72.
3. Elisabeth Elliot, *Let Me Be a Woman* (Wheaton: Living Books, 1976), 22.
4. Moore, *Living Beyond Yourself*, 72.

7

Loose Lips and Lying Tongues

This morning I received an e-mail containing untrue information from a friend who has a little problem being, well, overly dramatic. Less than an hour later she was calling me with an exaggerated piece of "breaking news." I did not reply to the e-mail or the phone message. Instead, I put my head in my hands and groaned. *We've got to stop this madness,* I thought as I rubbed my eyes. This friend needed to be talked to, and it wasn't going to be fun.

I'm sure you have had your fair share of experiences with the loose lips of those around you. And it is more than likely that you have been burned by someone else's lying tongue. It happens to the best of us at one time or another. But that does not make it right.

Although the phrase *Everyone is doing it* seems fitting enough when it comes to spreading rumors and gossiping, it does not give us an excuse to give in when we're the ones with the urge to stretch the truth or let our mouths run when we should keep them tightly shut. Matthew 12:36 tells us that we will be held accountable for absolutely everything we say. If that's not enough to shut our mouths, I don't know what is.

Any girl who desires to lead others and make a difference in the world around her can have an immediate impact in this area. In average teenage circles, it is likely that more gossip is exchanged than actual conversation. Recently my friend Shelby, who is a freshman, asked a group of us if we thought people ever talked about her behind her back when she walked by them at school.

My friend Amanda, who is older and out of high school, quickly answered, "Of course they do—it's high school." Shelby silently nodded at her response, and no one protested the probability of Amanda's statement. But the true question at the center of this issue should not be about how often we are the *focal point* of a conversation like that. Rather, it should be how often we are a *participant* in a conversation like that. Almost every girl I meet tells me that she has had problems with friends who talked about her behind her back or made up lies about her. But when asked, most of those same girls admit they have also been that kind of "friend" at one point or another.

First Timothy 4:12 says "Let no one look down on your youthfulness, but rather in speech, conduct, love, faith and purity, show yourself an example of those who believe." In other chapters we have discussed the importance of living out our faith in regard to conduct and purity. The other books in the BEING A GIRL series have at length examined the importance of love and faith. But we would miss the mark if we never discussed how much our words affect the way we are perceived by those around us and how *God* is perceived by those same people as a result.

A LONG LOOK IN THE MIRROR

Have you ever realized that you have never seen your own face? Because of the way your eyes are set in your head, it is impossible. You have only been able to see a *reflection* of your face in a mirror or an *image* of your face in a photograph. You rely on that reflection or image to show you what you really look like.

Imagine what you would think of yourself if the only mirror you ever saw was a fun-house mirror, where your body looked extra wide or your face looked super long. It would not mean that you really looked like that, but you would have a distorted idea of what you look like due to that incorrect reflection.

As Christians we are Christ's reflection, His workmanship. No one on earth at this time is going to see Jesus Christ in the flesh. We are as close as we will get to a human representation of Him. Marring Christ's reputation in the world is no small offense, yet we do it almost daily.

I once knew a girl who had a real problem with lying. She lied so much that I am not even sure whether she knew she was lying or not. Most of the time, she probably wouldn't have recognized the truth if it had jumped out and bitten her on the nose. One time, while hanging out at her house, I noticed a plaque hanging on the wall with a Bible verse on it. It created a lot of confusion in me because I could not understand how someone could outwardly proclaim one thing but choose to blatantly live another. Had I relied on her to be a portrait of Christ, or had I been weaker in my faith, I would have quit being a Christian altogether.

Our words are no small matter. They have the power to alter eternity. Another person's perception of the gospel message can be hinged on the things we choose to say. I know we won't be perfect, and ultimately we are not responsible for the eternal choices someone else makes, but it is still vitally important that we choose our words wisely. As I mentioned before, Scripture says that we will be held accountable for everything we say. That indicates that God takes this issue very seriously.

FORGET STICKS AND STONES—WORDS HURT!

All of us have heard the children's saying, "Sticks and stones may break my bones, but words will never hurt me." But nothing could be further from the truth. Broken bones usually heal far more quickly than broken hearts do. I don't remember many of the physical injuries I incurred growing up, but I sure have vivid memories of many emotional ones. It would probably be safe to say that I can remember more hurtful comments I have received over the years than compliments I got. The same is probably true for you.

My friend Ann's four-year-old daughter came home from school one day asking if she could get a nose job. She said she planned on saving her allowance to pay for it. When Ann asked her why she wanted a nose job, little Megan solemnly told her that the children in her preschool class told her she had a big nose. From that moment on Megan became obsessed with her nose. Her desire to get a nose job did not dissolve overnight either. She was haunted by her "big" nose. Truthfully, her nose wasn't big at all. But because someone else told her it was, she took it to heart and believed it to be true. How sad.

Almost all of us are insecure by nature. We have flaws we don't want others to notice and strengths we desperately hope they see. We crave their compliments and crumble at their criticism. Unlike a physical assault, verbal attacks are often played over and over again in our minds, gaining momentum and power each time. Sometimes, even long after the people who made the remarks have left our lives, we remember the things they said to us. Almost every memory we have is somehow associated with words.

Why is it that words hurt so much? It's been said that "I am not who I think I am. I am not who you think I am. I am who I think you think I am." That means we base our sense of self-worth on what others think of us, and we perceive what they think of us on the basis of what they *say* about us, just like little Megan did with her classmates. If others tell us we are ugly, they may not convince us that we really are ugly, but they most certainly will plant questions in our minds. We'll start wondering why they said it and questioning whether we are or not. Words are powerful.

If words have this much power over us, they must also have this much power over those around us. Yet we very rarely think of another person's feelings when he or she becomes the target of a gossip fest or the center of a campus-wide rumor. Most of the time we are so relieved someone else is the target that we join in spreading the gossip simply to avoid becoming a target ourselves. Girls who desire to lead others and exemplify Christ, however, must take ownership for their words and how they affect others. They must choose the words they use carefully.

Our mouths should be tools of encouragement and not discouragement. In his book *The Five Love Languages*, Gary Chapman writes: "The word *encourage* means 'to inspire courage.' All of us have areas in which we feel insecure. We lack courage, and that lack of courage often hinders us from accomplishing the positive things we would like to do."[1]

Do you tend to be the type of girl who inspires courage in those around you? Or do you tend to look for areas in which others are already insecure and make them feel even more vulnerable and rejected?

In junior high I hung out with a group of girls who were very catty and really mean. I don't know if I ever heard a genuine compliment come out of any of their mouths—or mine. Although I cannot speak for the other girls, I can tell you that I attacked others mostly because of my own insecurities. If one of the other girls looked better than I did on any given day, I knew I could convince her that she really didn't if I planted a seed of doubt in her mind with my words and the words of other jealous girls around me. I could use the same tactics with a girl who was getting attention from a boy I liked or who was doing better than I was in school. It wasn't right, but it worked. What I never stopped to consider was how my behavior exposed something about me that was truly ugly: a jealous and hateful heart.

GOSSIP CAN'T PROTECT

Gossip always starts with a heart that is jealous or hurt. The intention of gossip is always to hurt someone else—either someone who has hurt you or someone who is deemed a threat. Gossip continues traveling through the mouths of other jealous people *and* the mouths of those who are trying to protect the one who is hurt. In gossip, we are either trying to protect ourselves by making someone else look bad or we are trying to protect someone we love by passing on information about the person who wants to hurt or has already hurt our friend. In the latter case, jealousy masks itself as a *protecting friend*.

"I just wanted to let you know your best friend was talking bad about you," someone might say. "I would want to know if someone was doing it to me." But in most cases this "friend" is jealous of the friendship you and your best friend have and wants to see it come to a screeching halt.

In Christian circles we like to dress gossip up as prayer requests. They might sound something like this: "My friend Sarah is dating a non-Christian and I think they are having sex. She might be pregnant so we need to pray for her." Many times there is barely any element of truth in these "prayer requests." Poor Sarah might have been seen at the library with her science partner, who is not a Christian. And although there is nothing else going on between them, her reputation just got dragged through the mud.

Gossip is *never* for the good of another person, no matter how much we think it might be. Stopping gossip is always what is best. The e-mail I received this morning was from a friend who was trying to protect me. "You won't believe what they were going to try to do to hurt you," she wrote. What she had to say was an overly inflated version of a comment made a long, long time ago. What she was speaking as a fact was not even anywhere near the truth.

Her intentions were good, but that did not make her gossiping right. Passing on gossip always does more harm than good because it perpetuates a destructive cycle. If someone we know is out to hurt someone else we know, we first need to go to the one who has the bad intentions and try to stop them. Otherwise, what we are passing on is mere hearsay and speculation; it might not even be true. In that case, we are not only passing on gossip—we are also telling a lie.

> *Gossip is never for the good of another person.*

Years ago, my friend "Melanie" came to me to tell me our friend "Bryce" had plans to thwart a project I was working hard on. He wanted to see me fail because then he would have the leading project within our program. What she said turned out to be true, but the information was not helpful to me. You see, it made me angry at Bryce, but I was unable to explain my hostility to Bryce or anyone else without dragging Melanie (as the source of my information) into it. Since she was the one who heard all of these mean remarks straight from Bryce's lips, I encouraged her to speak with him. But she always seemed to chicken out, making me equally angry at her.

The result was that I felt betrayed by two friends. If she was telling the truth, why wouldn't she do anything about it? There was nothing I could do because all I had to go on was mere hearsay. By the time Melanie actually took the opportunity to talk with Bryce, it was too late. He had already put into motion his plan that destroyed his relationship with me. The surprising part in all of this was the strain created in Melanie's relationship with both Bryce and me. She could have saved a lot of heartache, and a friendship, had she chosen to confront Bryce in the first place rather than gossip about him behind his back.

Gossip destroys relationships because it always pits people against one another. It always divides—even though it may appear in the beginning to be something that will bring unity. You know what I am talking about. You and your friends choose to gang up on one girl, and the rest of you feel united in your stance against her. What you don't realize is that those very same friends can—and most likely will—turn on you sometime just as quickly as you all turned on that other girl. So your "unity" is always tenuous at best.

Gossip does not protect and it does not unite—not ever. Many times it masquerades as unity and friendship to lure you into its evil grasp. But those who gossip about others are almost always gossiped about, often by the very people they are gossiping with about other people.

And just like the childhood game Telephone, items of gossip usually grow in intensity and exaggeration the more they are passed around. People will add and remove things in translation, thus changing an already distorted message. By the end, the information may not bear any resemblance to the original; it becomes a complete and total rumor. And that is even worse than gossip.

When Rumors Start Flying

A friend of mine ran for student government shortly before her senior year of high school. Just before elections, the rumors started to fly on her small *Christian* school campus. Obscene things were written about her on bathroom stall walls, and notes containing false statements were passed in the hallway. She overheard two girls talking about her behind her back in the bathroom when they didn't know she was there.

Apparently there was even a boy who stood at the ballot box and told everyone who voted for her to change their vote. Because of running for this office, her reputation got smeared for no good reason at all. The rumors were the worst of it. As a pastor's daughter, the rumors made up about her were especially vicious and damaging. Someone went so far as to say that my friend and her parents used church tithe money to pay for her new car. (In reality, her car was a gift from someone outside of her family.) I don't know what it is about human nature, but we like to believe the worst about other people. I'd like to think that Christians are above this kind of mean-spirited behavior, but experience has taught me otherwise.

I spoke at another Christian school several months ago, and afterward a girl approached me with a poem she had written about gossip. She was new at the school, and because she came from a rougher home than most of the other students, someone started a rumor that she was bisexual. One of the administrators told me he heard that it was a fact.

After talking with this girl and seeing the embarrassment and humiliation in her eyes, I came to the conclusion that the rumor was a cruel lie spread by jealous girls. The new girl was absolutely gorgeous, and the other girls probably didn't want to have to compete with her for the attention of the limited pool of guys on campus.

This girl ended her note to me with a quote by Eleanor Roosevelt: "Great minds discuss ideas; Average minds discuss events; Small minds discuss people."[2] I am almost certain that none of us desires to be known as shallow. Yet many times we lower ourselves to that category without even thinking twice.

So how do we stop this problem? How do we stand up and lead others out of gossip and back to the truth? The answer is easier said than done. We simply think *before* we speak.

RECOGNIZING WHAT IS GOSSIP

In his book *Stop the Runaway Conversation*, Dr. Michael D. Sedler refers to all gossip as "an evil report." And he came up with eight ways to identify whether or not the person you are conversing with is an evil reporter.[3] Let's look at those eight points and what they look like in the lives of average teenage girls.

1. "The messenger will look for support from you for her beliefs, attitudes or actions."

This is what happens when someone comes to you and says something like, "Don't you think Jayne is annoying? She is so loud and obnoxious, and she always tries to steal all of the attention." This is a gossiper's equivalent of knocking on your door to see if anyone is home; she's testing to see if she is welcome to come in and throw a gossip party.

If you do not open this door, you will be able to avoid gossip. Do not give a gossiper ground to lure you in so you can gossip together. Dodge her questions or blatantly shut her down. Say something like, "I happen to like Jayne. She is one of my closest friends," or "We all have our moments when we can be loud or annoying." If you do this a few times, the gossiper will likely get the message that you don't want to play this game.

Also, make it a point to watch your own speech to see if you begin sentences this way. Stop yourself midsentence if you suddenly realize what you're doing. Break this habit, and you will curtail the gossip habits in your life fairly quickly.

2. *"Messengers with an evil report will try to distract you from a God-given focus or course of action."*

As girls who desire to lead and make a difference in the world around us, we know that we need to flee gossip. Many times we will even ask our friends to hold us accountable to this noble task. But be aware that when we try to establish stronger spiritual patterns in our own lives, some of our friends won't want to rise to that standard, and they'll try to pull us back down.

Here's an example of how this might look. Let's say you have mentioned to your best friend that you are trying to stop gossiping. Feeling uncomfortable, she might try to justify her gossip to you the next time you talk. It could sound something like this, "I heard Julie isn't going to play softball this year. *This isn't gossip* because you need to know. If she doesn't play, it gives you a shot at being the starting catcher, you know? She was never that good anyway."

Don't be fooled; this still qualifies as gossip and hearsay. Your friend is still in the wrong, but she doesn't want to be in the wrong alone—she wants to bring you with her. In moments like this it is so important that you hold fast to your convictions and say something like, "I appreciate your looking out for me, but it is still gossip. If Julie's not going to play anymore, I would rather hear it from her or the coach. Thanks for letting me know, but next time I would appreciate it if you just kept this news to yourself."

Pay close attention to your own words in conversation, making sure that you don't try to draw others into gossip after they have been convicted of it and are actively trying to change. You need to ask yourself before sharing something if the information is true, necessary, and fair. If not, whether it can be justified or not, it is still gossip.

3. *"One who carries a false report will attempt to create disunity and division."*

We talked about this a bit already. This is where you see friends pitted against other friends. I'm sure you know the routine. This usually happens within a tight group of friends or on some sort of team. If you sing on the worship team for your youth group, a friend might come to you and tell you that "Katie thinks you sing like a squawking chicken."

She does this to drive a wedge between you and Katie, and quite possibly even to elevate herself to the position of soloist. Beware any time someone comes to you with a comment that will pit you against someone else. And make it a point not to divide friends with your words either.

4. *"An individual who conveys negative reports often shows anger when you disagree with her."*

People who become angry or emotional when we do not agree with them are usually out for personal gain somehow. They are looking to feel validated. If Kim comes to you to share something negative about Tanya, and you stop her and remind her that Tanya is one of your best friends, you will usually be able to judge by Kim's reaction whether she came to you with the intention of gossiping.

If she responds by saying something like, "You're right. I'm sorry. I shouldn't talk about her like that," then you know she just got caught up in the heat of an emotional moment as we all tend to do, and you can help set her back on the right track.

However, if she gets defensive and begins to defend herself with remarks like, "But you don't know what she did to me," then you know she has a definite motive for gossip and you need to (gently) stop her in her tracks. Refuse to jump on someone else's bad-news bandwagon. And when someone has hurt you, do not go looking for recruits to join you in the hurt and disgruntled club. Deal with your issues privately, before the Lord, without dragging others into them.

5. *"A messenger sharing information that will violate your spirit will often approach you with an apparently demure and modest attitude."*

I really like how Dr. Sedler explains this one. He says, "By appearing to need your advice and guidance, she might portray herself as unable to figure something out. This is very common for the experienced carrier of an evil report. 'Could I ask your opinion on something?'

"While this sounds innocent, your nod of approval will generally bring an onslaught of gossip: 'Yesterday Jenny did something really awful. She went to this movie and ...' If you do not stop the forward progression of gossip right away your curiosity will be aroused and, before you know it, you will have listened to an evil report about Jenny."[4]

When people come to you for opinions, make sure the things they are seeking opinions on are worth your attention. You don't want to be merely a "dumping ground" for their negative feelings and thoughts. In the same way, when you seek other people's opinions, make sure you are not looking for a way to simply drop a gossip bomb.

6. *"A transporter of negative information will attempt to show off his power, strength or authority."* Many girls try to throw the weight of their popularity around. They try to lure you into gossip by promising friendship and popularity if you will build up their egos and tear down those they do not like. It is easy to get caught in this trap since none of us want to be torn down and seen as unpopular.

In moments like these you need to remember that popularity has a price tag; many times you have to pay for it with your integrity. And that is never a fair trade. If you find yourself in a situation where you have to engage in gossip in order to maintain your popularity ... don't do it. Give up the popularity—any girl who leads does not want to be popular at that price. And whatever you do, do not throw around your own popularity by trying to get people to jump on your own gossip bandwagon.

7. *"The individual will flatter and praise you."* Many times people will try to butter someone up before they ask for something. My husband likes to tease me and tell me I do this before I ask if I can buy something expensive. We have all done it as kids—we tell our parents they are the best, and then ask if we can do something we think they would otherwise oppose. Not all compliments are manipulative, but some truly are.

Be on the lookout for friends who will butter you up with compliments—"Cute hair." "Awesome purse!"—and then try to lure you into something like gossip. Refuse to be manipulated by flattery. And do not use flattery as a weapon to gain what you want either.

High school can be summed up in one word: drama.

8. *"The messenger of an evil report will often embellish and exaggerate a situation to make it seem worse than it really is."* This is very common, especially when you are dealing with girls. Most of the time high school can be summed up in one word: drama. The high school girls I have worked with always said that they were looking forward to graduating and getting away from all of that drama. Some people, though, tend to bring drama with them wherever they go.

If someone comes to you and starts in on a huge and dramatic story, do both of you a favor and stop them (no matter how entertaining the story might be). Life does not need to be that dramatic. And in most cases it isn't that dramatic. Drama is a key sign in identifying gossip. So avoid drama at all costs. A true princess has no business acting like a drama queen.

LIKE A MATCH

Most of us do not realize the amount of harm our tongues can cause. The human tongue is like a match—if you light it, it can take down an entire forest. That is why what we say is so important. Gossip is a very normal and common thing, but that does not make it right. That is why those who choose not to gossip, or listen to others gossip, will emerge as leaders. The same is true of lying and overly dramatizing the facts.

The next time you find yourself wanting to add or take away a fact or two from a story you are repeating, catch yourself. Even the slightest alteration can turn the truth into a lie. If "everybody's doing it" when it comes to lying and gossip, then those who don't will soon stand out. So next time your tongue feels like going for a run, grab it, hold it, and save yourself a lot of heartache and trouble.

FOR FURTHER THOUGHT:

1. Are you more prone to be one who spreads gossip or the one who listens to it? Why do you think that is?

2. Which of the eight identifiers do you have the hardest time with? Why?

3. What are some practical ways you can stop yourself from gossiping?

4. Do you have a tendency to add to or take away from a story to add impact? How can you stop yourself from continuing this pattern?

5. Is overcoming gossip and lying something that is easy or difficult for you? Why do you think that is?

LEADERSHIP IN ACTION:

As you go through your day, make a mental list of all of the times you are tempted to either spread gossip or listen to it. At the end of the day make an actual list of all of the things you were tempted to gossip about. Divide the list into categories and find the area where you seem to struggle most. Try to determine why that is and how you can combat it. For instance, if you notice you are tempted to gossip about a pretty girl more than once a day, you might find that you are jealous and you don't even realize it. By dealing with your jealousy (the root of your problem), it might help you curtail your urge to gossip.

Notes

1. Gary Chapman, *The Five Love Languages* (Chicago: Northfield Publishing, 1992), 42.
2. *http://en.thinkexist.com/quotation/great_minds_discuss_ideas-average_minds_discuss/166649.html* (accessed June 13, 2005).
3. Michael D. Sedler, *Stop the Runaway Conversation* (Grand Rapids: Chosen Books, 2001), 24–31.
4. Ibid., 28.

8

Lessons From a Dirty Band-Aid

During my sophomore year at a Christian university, one of my floor mates plopped onto the futon in my dorm room and began to tell me about how many of her friends were beginning to take part in a new kind of sexual revolution.

"It's not just about sex anymore," she said. "People are doing everything but sex, and they are thinking that makes it okay." I nodded my head as I listened; I was trying to remove some of the clutter from my small dresser as she talked to me. Finally I just opened the top drawer and began tossing things inside.

"My friends in high school used to say they were doing it for experience," I said, still focused on the monstrous task of organizing my stuff. I blew a stray strand of hair out of my face and turned to face my friend on the couch. "They told me they were experimenting sexually so they wouldn't feel stupid on their wedding night," I continued. My friend burst out laughing and quickly covered her mouth to stifle the sound.

"Are you serious?" She raised her eyebrows and waited for my reply. Just then I decided to run my arm along the top of my dresser, sweeping all of my junk out of sight and into the top drawer. But by doing so I cut my arm on the edge of my dresser and a small red line appeared on my arm.

"Ouch," I said, ignoring her question. "I'm bleeding and I'm out of Band-Aids. You don't happen to have one, do you?"

She shook her head slowly. "Just the one I'm wearing," she added, holding up her injured index finger.

"You're gross," I said, scrunching my nose. I joined her on the futon with a tissue pressed to my arm, trying to stop the bleeding. "But brilliant," I added. When she responded with a quizzical look, I shared the analogy that I'm about to share with you now.

A BAND-AID WITH A RÉSUMÉ

When I cut my arm that day I wanted a clean Band-Aid. I didn't want a Band-Aid with a résumé full of experience. I didn't want the one on my friend's finger. I wanted one that would keep *me* from bleeding. In the heat of the moment, when it really mattered to me, the Band-Aid that covered Lindsay's burn mark or concealed Katie's skinned knee wasn't even worth considering. I don't think I need to work hard to convince you that using someone else's dirty Band-Aid on your fresh wound would be downright disgusting.

But it's a mentality that many Christians are taking on today. As more and more teens are taking part in a sexual revolution of sorts, they find themselves becoming like used Band-Aids, trying to boast about their experiences. Over the years I have met many girls who have compromised their purity, and although each of them has a different story, many of them sound the same.

A lot of girls claim that making out and letting their hands wander (or letting guys' hands wander all over them) is not that big of a deal. They view it as an exciting time to try new things. Some have told me this way they will be "experienced" when they fall in love and are ready to go all the way. But if experience is not what you are looking for in a Band-Aid, why would it be what you are looking for in a life mate?

This sexual exploration is *not* stopping at kissing and touching. Teens across this nation have been caught in school bathrooms, on school buses, and in church closets (not to mention the backseats of cars) stripping down and having a new kind of sex. What they are doing isn't intercourse, and they cannot get pregnant from doing it, so they think they are okay. This mentality has spawned the new term "technical virginity," which is used to define someone who has not had sexual intercourse but is nevertheless sexually active.

I hear from girls all the time who are under the assumption that this behavior isn't sex, but I disagree. Anything that involves the intimate places of your body being touched in a sexual way is sex. Sure, it may not be intercourse, but it's still something that should not be happening between any two people who aren't married.

HOW MANY PEOPLE WILL SHARE YOUR BED?

Some day in the future, on your wedding night, do you want to climb into bed for your first night of romance wondering about all of the times in the past that "weren't that big of a deal" to your husband? Do you want to be compared to all of the other girls he has "experienced"? If you're honest, you answered no to both of those questions.

In college, a few months before a friend of mine was to be married, she woke me up in the middle of the night in tears. It was several moments before she could speak, so I went into the kitchen and made some tea while she tried to calm herself down. I glanced at her ring and saw that it was still there, so I knew she hadn't called the wedding off. I couldn't imagine what else could be so traumatic. What she told me next broke my heart.

She and her fiancé had just had a long talk about their past relationships (why they waited until this point I do not know), and he told her he was not a virgin; in tears he apologized for not waiting. My friend had waited, and she was devastated. She felt like she had been cheated and robbed of the one thing that was rightly hers. Only a wife should know her husband intimately and sexually, but she would have to share this knowledge with an ex-girlfriend who would always haunt her like a phantom.

Yes, there is restoration and renewal for those who have fallen. We will talk more about that in a minute. But the one thing better than being sexually restored is *remaining* sexually whole. As a virgin who married a virgin, I can tell you there was such joy and relief in knowing that sex was something both my husband and I would share only with each other.

In 1996, the most credible sexual study undertaken to date was made available to the public by the University of Chicago. Some of its findings included:

- People who reported being most physically pleased (by sex) and emotionally satisfied were married couples.
- Lowest rates of satisfaction were among men and women who were neither married nor living with someone—the very group thought to be having the hottest sex.
- Physical and emotional satisfaction started to decline when people had more than one sexual partner.[1]

There are other studies that claim that those who have premarital sex are more likely to divorce. Youth leaders I had growing up used to warn us of the consequences of premarital sex by sharing their stories. Many of them told us that stupid mistakes they made in high school robbed them of some of the pleasures of sex in marriage because they were tormented by old memories and comparisons.

Sin is sin, just like black is black. But the Bible tells us that sexual sin is different from any other sin in one way: We are sinning against our own bodies. First Corinthians 6:18 says, "Flee sexual immorality. Every sin that a man does is outside the body, but he who commits sexual immorality sins against his own body" (NKJV). Every time you are tempted to engage in premarital sex, remind yourself of the dirty Band-Aid. If you think that is disgusting, picture yourself exchanging bodily fluids with someone who has exchanged bodily fluids with lots of other people.

That's even more disgusting. Even if the guy you are contemplating having sex with is a virgin, if he is not your husband, you should not be engaging in any sexual acts with him. That is what the Bible means when it says, "Flee sexual immorality."

When the Going Gets Tough

When my husband and I were in premarital counseling, the couple we met with warned us about how hard it would be to stay pure until our wedding night—no matter how committed to purity we were. Jan, the wife, said, "You will get to a point where it will feel and seem right because it will be right very, very soon. As you prepare for a future together you will begin to function like a unit. You will begin to become one in many ways, but you need to make sure you don't do what *seems* right and you do what *is* right. What is right is waiting for marriage."

She was right. Michael and I were functioning together as one. We were looking for an apartment that we would live in together once we were married. We registered for items that would furnish our household. We planned a trip to Hawaii for our honeymoon. The closer we got, the more it began to seem like *we were already married*. We recognized that we could fall into sexual sin just as easily as anyone else, so we made a rule. If we were at either of our houses, we could not be there alone.

If no one else was home, we had to go out for the day or evening. Sure, when others were home we would sit in the living room and watch a movie alone, but there was always the possibility that someone else would come walking into the room at any minute. And at night, if other family members began to go off to bed, we ended our night too, so we wouldn't be the only ones awake in the house late at night. These simple guidelines really helped us to stay pure.

On one occasion, no one was going to be home at either of our houses and we didn't really want to go out. So Michael called his sister and brother-in-law and invited them over for the evening. We all met up at Michael's house and hung out for the night. They teased us about needing "baby-sitters," but being newly married, they understood our plight.

Things can heat up really quickly.

No one is above falling, so you need to be wise about the situations in which you place yourself. Do not put yourself in a dangerous circumstance. You should never be alone with a guy. Things can heat up really quickly, and before you know it you might be doing something you will later regret.

In an article entitled "Straight From a Guy," which was published in *BRIO* magazine, Rory Partin shares a story I found absolutely shocking. He said:

> One of my Christian friends got pregnant in her boyfriend's hospital room after he was recovering from a terrible car accident that left him partially paralyzed. Sounds impossible, huh? I'm telling you—guys are wired like sexual time bombs. That's simply how God created men.
>
> And, yes, it's our responsibility to be wise and stay out of stupid situations where we're alone and will battle temptation, but we guys need your help. You can actually help us keep our thoughts and actions pure by suggesting we do stuff in groups instead of being alone. When you dress modestly,

we're not thinking, *Where'd she find that—Goodwill?* Believe me, we're thinking, *Whew! Finally, a girl who's smart enough not to flaunt it.* Seriously, I promise *that's* what we are thinking.[2]

Guys just think differently than we do. But we can get caught up in the moment just like they can. It takes two people to fall into sexual sin. When the going gets tough and you think you might fall, it's best that you flee the situation as quickly as possible.

NO CONDEMNATION IN CHRIST JESUS

Perhaps you are feeling condemned as you read this because it is too late for you to remain a virgin. Condemnation is not my goal. I simply long for each girl who reads this book to know how big of a deal sex is. The Lord can restore those who have fallen into sexual sin, just like He can restore those of us who fall into other kinds of sin. It's the reason He went to the cross.

Psalm 51:7 says, "Wash me, and I shall be whiter than snow." That is what the Lord does for us when we repent; He washes us whiter than snow. He cannot go back and give us the purity we gave away, but He can make us pure from this day forward and give us a second virginity of sorts. If you are reading this book in brokenness, simply ask the Lord for forgiveness. Ask Him to make you whiter than snow.

Confess your sin before Him, and leave your past behind you. Go to a youth leader or another trusted adult and ask for their help to make the necessary changes in your life. If you are in an impure relationship, get out of it. Don't feel like you have to stay with someone just because you gave him your virginity. Do not stay in a situation that is both tempting and harmful. Come clean before God and hold out for a guy who will make your purity a priority in his life. Let today be the first day of your second virginity.

Perhaps your brokenness comes from being the victim of a sexual crime. If you have been raped or molested in your past, please know that I am so sorry. God does not look on you as impure or unclean. In His eyes you are still very much a virgin. Please do not condemn yourself for circumstances that were beyond your control.

Let the Lord heal your hurts and make you whole again. Walk boldly in the knowledge that you are still pure in His sight. If this has happened to you, I strongly suggest you get counseling from someone in your church so you can talk through the pain this experience has caused you. Things like this are always easier when you have someone you can talk openly with, someone who will share the burden with you through prayer.

The Pain Behind the Problem

Maybe you are wondering what kind of church I attend if I think sex is a problem with Christian teens. Perhaps you have not been exposed to this sexual revolution taking place in Christian circles. You wear a purity ring with pride and would not even think about having any kind of sex before your wedding night. If so . . . good for you!

But just because you don't *see* a certain problem does not mean it is not there or that it will not affect you in some way someday. Remember my friend in college who waited but her husband didn't? She was shocked to find that things were not as she had expected them to be. Don't be quick to judge those who are involved in sexual activity. Try to understand the thinking behind what they do, and see if you can be a tool in God's hand to pull them out of such a sad and empty lifestyle.

Almost every time I speak at an event I meet a girl who has compromised her own purity or is devastated by a good Christian friend who has. This is a problem that sweeps across the denominational board and is rampant in public schools and private Christian schools alike. Why is it such a problem?

I once sat across the table from a thirteen-year-old girl who had been caught in sexual activity, and I asked her if it was worth it. Defiantly she told me what she had done was "no big deal." This same girl, who regularly attends church with her family and has attended both Christian and public schools, claims to be a Christian, yet she also told me she has "made out" with other girls. When I asked her if she considered herself to be a lesbian, she said, "No, it was just something to do."

As I began to gently point out the dangers and consequences of what she had done, she glared at me. When I quietly asked her how what she had done made her feel about herself, she sat in silence as tears rolled down her cheeks. She wanted love and acceptance, and she was looking for it everywhere. The trouble was, she was finding it nowhere.

It's been said that "guys will give love for sex, and girls will give sex for love." That is a very true statement. After a purity event I spoke at a year or so ago, a thin girl with dark eyeliner walked up to my book table and thrust a note into my hands.

"This is for you; read it later," she said quickly without looking me in the eye, and abruptly left. What I read later that night broke my heart. She had written me a ten-page letter explaining her story. With an abusive father, who eventually left the family, this girl had no role model of what a man should be. In early middle school she began to kiss boys and experiment by touching them in inappropriate ways and letting them touch her anywhere and everywhere. In high school, she began to sleep around.

When her reputation at school got so tarnished that none of the guys would sleep with her, she began to go on Internet chat rooms and meet older men who would later meet her in a parking lot somewhere. They would have sex in the backseat of cars.

"I don't do it to be popular or to fit in. I don't feel peer pressure to have sex," she wrote in her letter. "I have sex because it is *the one thing I can offer that will make someone love me.*" She signed her letter "Violated Girl." She also left an e-mail address, but when I sent her an e-mail she did not respond. I wasn't surprised; she had already told me that someone like me could never understand the depth of her pain.

Desperately Looking for Love

Whether girls who are having sex do it because of peer pressure, affection for a boyfriend, or to make up for a troubled past, they do it because they are looking for love. The world tells us that sex is love, but the Bible tells us something different. The Bible tells us that God is love (1 John 4:8).

> *They are looking for love in the wrong place.*

Girls who are sexually experimental are not finding the love and satisfaction they are looking for because they are looking for love in the wrong place. To me, the saddest part of this reality is that Christian girls are among those searching. They have heard the truth about love, but they are not convinced.

That means that those of us who are claiming we are Christians are not accurately portraying the gospel in our lives. Sometimes we are even the rejecting forces that drive people to look for love outside of Christ and His church. The message of salvation is the greatest truth ever told; anyone who does not receive it really does not understand it. Sometimes the problem lies with them, but other times it lies with us. Too often, Christians come across as legalistic ("Here's a list of rules it takes to be a Christian") or judgmental ("You've got to clean up your act before coming to Christ"). When we shun those looking for love, it's easy for them to think that Jesus is shunning them too.

A lot of girls who desire to change cannot do so without help. They don't know how. Many girls—even girls attending youth group—come from homes where they feel unloved. Some have parents who are very poor role models. Some girls do not grow up having a strong foundation of right and wrong. The best way to treat those who have fallen is to *love them in spite of their sin*. You do not have to accept their sin, and you can be vocal about why you think it is wrong. But you need to bring your message to them in a loving way, making sure that you always communicate acceptance of them as people when you oppose their sinful behavior.

What did Jesus say to the woman caught in adultery? What did He do when the religious people gathered to condemn her? John chapter 8 tells us that He bent down to write in the dirt. What did He write? The Bible does not tell us. But whatever it was, it caused them to walk away. Perhaps Jesus started writing *their* sins in the dirt for the public to read.

"He who is without sin among you, let him be the first to throw a stone at her," He said (John 8:7). And when her accusers left, Jesus turned to the woman and asked, "Woman, where are they? Did no one condemn you?" She said, "No one, Lord." And Jesus said, "I do not condemn you, either. Go. From now on sin no more" (John 8:10–11).

When we begin to condemn others for the sexual sins they have committed and we begin to elevate ourselves to a position where we think, *I will never do that,* Jesus comes to us and says, "If you have never sinned, then go ahead and judge." None of us is free from sin outside of Jesus Christ. So if sexual sin is an area that you do not struggle with, be thankful for that. But be gentle with those who do struggle. You can let them know they are living in sin, but please do not make them feel like they are beyond God's love and forgiveness.

BAND-AIDS ON BINDERS

I have shared the message contained in this chapter at many youth events across this nation. Every time I share it, I get an influx of e-mails right away. Many girls have told me the analogy of a dirty Band-Aid has given them a real wake-up call. Some even go as far as sticking Band-Aids on their binders and bathroom mirrors to remind them of their commitment to purity. In college, after I cut my arm and discovered this analogy, I stuck a Band-Aid to my mirror above my dresser. It was a great conversation piece every time I had a visitor.

The truth is, none of us wants to be like a dirty Band-Aid. We desire to be wanted and loved, not tossed aside like a used Band-Aid. And as much as we want to be clean Band-Aids, we also want to marry clean Band-Aids. So as you work toward and fight for your own purity, pray for the purity of the man you will one day marry. I spent ten years of my life praying for Michael before I ever knew him, and when God brought us together, he was the answer to all of my prayers and more. As you wait on your life mate, be for him what you want him to be for you. Live each day with purposeful resolve to be a clean Band-Aid.

FOR FURTHER THOUGHT:

1. What is it that grosses you out about the concept of using someone else's dirty Band-Aid? How can that same principle apply to having premarital sexual encounters?

2. What are some firm boundaries you can set to ensure that you remain pure until your wedding night?

3. Make a list of things you consider to be off-limits before marriage (sex, making out, inappropriate touching, being alone, etc.) and a list of things you consider to be within the limits

before marriage (holding hands, hugging, playing footsie, etc.). If you are in a small group, discuss your answers and rethink your second list. Are there any dangers on this list that need to be moved to the off-limits one?

4. What are some ways you can reach out to friends or girls you know who are involved in sinful lifestyles without compromising your own standards?

5. Make a list of traits you want your future husband to have, stick it somewhere you will see it often, and pray over that list regularly.

LEADERSHIP IN ACTION:

I used to think purity contracts were cheesy, but I did have a purity ring. When Michael and I were engaged, we attended a marriage conference where we were encouraged to sign a purity covenant, so we did. And it was a cool experience for us.

Outlining your boundaries and having a tangible way (like a contract or ring) to remind yourself of your commitment to purity can be a really good thing. Take some time to pray about your purity and sign the contract below that pledges your commitment to stay pure from now until your wedding day. (It doesn't matter whether you have been pure up until this point or not— you can still sign the pledge for your life from now on.)

Have a witness sign it with you so you have someone to keep you accountable to your commitment. Then take a Band-Aid and stick it somewhere you will see it. Let it serve as a vivid reminder of the importance of your commitment to purity.

The Dirty Band-Aid Purity Contract

I promise to honor God and my future husband in all of my actions. I will not engage in any form of sexual contact until my wedding night. I will make a conscious effort not to be alone with any guy, and I will guard my purity by making wise decisions.

I also commit to praying for the purity of my future husband on a regular and consistent basis. I do not want to be a dirty Band-Aid, and I do not desire to marry a dirty Band-Aid. From this day forward I promise to do my best to remain clean and pure.

X _____

X _____
    (Witness)

Date: _____

Notes

1. Robert T. Michael, John H. Gagnon, Edward O. Laumann, and Gina Kolata, *Sex in America* (Chicago: Univ. of Chicago Press), 124, as quoted in Dannah Gresh's *And the Bride Wore White* (Chicago: Moody, 1999).

2. Rory Partin, "Straight From a Guy," *BRIO* magazine, 2001, quoted at *www.premaritalsex.info/guy.htm* (accessed on June 13, 2005).

9

It's Not Just About Eating Your Vegetables

About two and half months before I got married, I decided to plan a date night. I called ahead and made arrangements to have him fitted for his tuxedo for the wedding at the beginning of the evening, and then we went out to a restaurant of his choice—which is rare since he usually lets me pick. It was designed to be a night about the two of us—a chance to take hold of a moment in our lives that was passing us by.

The man I planned the date for that night was *not* my husband-to-be. He was my dad. There was just something about preparing to get married and leaving my parents' household that made me realize all of the opportunities I had wasted. I had not done a good job at letting my parents know how much I appreciated them and how grateful I was for all they had done for me.

In Exodus 20:12 it clearly commands us to "Honor your father and your mother, that your days may be prolonged in the land which the Lord your God gives you." So many times we sell ourselves short when it comes to fulfilling this command. We assume that honoring our father and mother simply means obeying them when it comes to cleaning our rooms and eating our vegetables.

It is obvious that most girls today do *not* honor their parents in any way at all, much less the right way. Honoring our parents is not just about vegetables and clean bedrooms. In fact, it does not stop at obedience—although it does begin there. Since this is an area where so many girls are failing, it is a perfect opportunity for those aspiring to fulfill God's commandments and be a leader for Him to step up and make a difference.

I looked up the word *honor* and came across three definitions that offer us an incredible amount of insight into what fulfilling this command really means and how we can live it out in our daily lives. This chapter alone will probably be worth the price of the book to your parents, and it will be an incredible tool in helping you strengthen your relationship with them, no matter whether you get along with them right now or not.

THIS TIME IT IS ABOUT YOU

Before we even begin this discussion about what honoring our parents looks like, I want to address one thing that is sure to come up in the minds of some of you reading this book. *Shannon,* you might be thinking, *if you knew my parents, you would know that God certainly did not intend for me to fulfill this commandment. My parents are much too difficult and mean. They never do anything for me, and they love my brother or sister more anyway.*

I meet a lot of girls who express similar sentiments to me. Some of them have reasons to feel that way. However . . . honoring our parents is one of the Ten Commandments, which means *it is a command we all have to obey.* If you think you are exempt from having to obey it, you are sadly mistaken. Here's why: The same rationale you would use to say you do not have to honor your parents is the same rationale someone else could use to say they have the right to murder, steal, or commit adultery. According to God's Word, dishonoring our parents is no small offense. Just look at the other sins that surround this one—they are the big guns!

If honoring your parents is hard for you, take a moment and

stop looking at all of the things they have done wrong. Instead, look at the things they have done *right*. Chances are, they have put a roof over your head and fed you for at least some portion of your life. Your mom gave birth to you, even though abortion is a legalized option in this country. Maybe your parents take you to church or pay private school tuition so you can have a good education. Perhaps they even bought you this book. Changing your perspective on your parents might be all it takes to help you change your attitude about honoring them.

Now, I understand that you may come from a very painful situation and an unhappy home. Perhaps you even come from a broken family. I hear from countless girls who have been abandoned by one parent and feel like a misfit or a burden when one (or both) of their par-

> *Look at the things they have done* right.

ents remarry and start a blended or brand-new family. That's tough stuff. My husband comes from a blended family. Both of his parents were married before, and each had three kids in their previous marriage. When they married each other, they both had their final child—my husband. Although things have gone fairly smoothly for all of them, they would all attest to the fact that it has not been the Brady Bunch. There are certain pains and frustrations that they face simply because they are a blended family.

But whatever hurt you are experiencing does not give you a reason not to obey God's command. You are still to honor your father and your mother—and your stepfather and stepmother if you have them—simply because God tells you to, not because they have earned it.

Special Cases

Perhaps you have been a victim of sexual or physical abuse at the hand of a parent. I had a good friend in this situation. And if this is your story, I am so sorry. You never, ever have to do anything outside of God's will—and submitting to this type of abuse is *not* God's will. So please do not misunderstand what I am saying here. If you are in this type of situation or you have been there before, it is God's will for you to get out of that situation and to *stay* out of it. So please get the help you need.

It is not God's will for you to stay in any relationship that is sexually immoral or physically and psychologically harmful. Honoring your parents in this case would be found in pointing them toward God's truth, and you can do this best by holding them accountable for their actions. How do you do that? By getting out from under the abuse—leaving as quickly as you can. You can still honor your parents in your heart, from afar, and keep God's command without submitting to them up close where you could get hurt. Please, please, do not misunderstand me on this point.

In cases that do not involve abuse, however, each and every one of us *must* honor our parents and submit to their authority if we desire to honor God with our lives. This chapter is not about whether your parents are *worthy* of that love. It's about God's command for you to love them, whether they are worthy or not. After all, it was while you were still a sinner (and unworthy of His love) that Christ died for you (Romans 5:8).

A TOKEN OF YOUR AFFECTION

According to *dictionary.com*, one definition for *honor* is "a mark, token, or gesture of respect or distinction: *the place of honor at the table.*" When I took my dad out on a date a few months before my wedding, it was my way of honoring him for being the first man I ever loved and for doing a great job helping me get to the place I was at in my life.

When I first asked him out on that date at the dinner table one night, he was a little startled and taken aback. My dad and I are close, but neither of us could remember the last time we went out alone together. My dad and I aren't always the best at communicating with each other; I tend to communicate better with my mom since we are both big talkers.

But this time, at this special moment in my life, I knew I needed to reach out and acknowledge my dad and share a special moment with him before the opportunity was lost. I only wish I hadn't waited for a special occasion to create such an evening.

Your parents do a lot of things for you that you don't even realize. I spoke at a Christian school chapel recently where many of the kids tried to tell me that their parents don't care about them at all. Slowly, and a bit hesitantly at first, I began to ask them about the clothes and the shoes that they were wearing, their cell phones, their cars, the school supplies in their backpacks, and the tuition bills that got paid. Over 90 percent of the time those things were paid for by parents.

Several girls told me their dads work all of the time and are never home. One girl I met has a real bitterness toward her dad because of this. "He even takes side jobs on the weekends," she said to me angrily. Gently, I began to point out the fact that her family did not live extravagantly, so her dad probably had to work that hard in order to provide for the family.

This girl was wearing a nice letterman's jacket and was involved in an expensive extracurricular activity. I asked her if she ever thought once about how her dad worked six or seven days a week *in order for her to have those things*. She sat in silence and the firmness of her clinched jaw softened slightly in response.

For years I watched my own mom go without new clothes or new shoes so I could keep up on all of the latest trends. I always came first to her, and on days like Mother's Day and her birthday, I used to only find time to give a last-minute gift or a halfhearted sentiment. Most of the time, I simply let time get away from me when it came to preparing for such occasions. But then I began to realize that I didn't need special occasions to let my mom know that I love her.

It is more than likely that you have at least one parent who works harder than you even know and goes without at times so that you can have not only what you need but also what you want—and you don't even realize it. So many times the generous and giving hearts of our parents have been there for so long that we cannot remember a time when things weren't that way. This makes it easy for us to take our parents for granted.

That is why it is vitally important that we learn to take advantage of opportunities to honor them with respect and do something out of the ordinary for them. Your parents do not give to you so that they can get something in return. But more often than not, the little things you do for them mean more to them than they will ever be able to tell you. Doing the dishes for your mom when it's not your night to do them, or dusting the living room so she doesn't have to, could do wonders for her on a bad (or even a good) day.

Writing a little note to the dad you don't see often might be just what it takes to help him keep going when he gets burned out on the job. Bragging about your parents to someone else when you know your parents can overhear you might encourage them in ways you could never imagine. And taking your dad out on dates or your mom out for lunch and a day of shopping might help strengthen your relationship and create a memory that will last a lifetime. Look for a mark, a token, or a gesture of respect you can give your parents (and try to give them something or do something for them individually instead of doing something for them as a couple). Don't wait for a special occasion. Just do it.

WHAT'S IN A NAME?

In a previous chapter I mentioned how having the last name Kubiak used to mean that I was a reflection on my parents. Apparently those who write the dictionary agree with me, because another definition for the word *honor* is a "good name; reputation." In a very literal sense, you are your parents' reputation. Even if you do not have the same last name as your parents, you are still a reflection on them. How successful (or unsuccessful) they are as parents is determined by your attitude and actions.

There are many girls I have met over the years that I walk away from wondering, *Where did those parents go wrong?* Now, a parent cannot always be to blame when it comes to having a terrible child, but they usually have at least something to do with it. The same goes for those whose children turn out wonderful.

No matter how you may feel about your parents at times, it is highly important that you realize and recognize that you hold not only your reputation (and sometimes God's reputation), but also your parents' reputations in your hands. That is no small task. Work hard at giving them a great reputation and a name that is highly esteemed.

You need to be careful not to fall into a performance trap, though, like I did growing up. Because my dad is so nonverbal, I used to think I needed to work extra hard to win his love. I always tried to excel in sports, academics, and other extracurricular activities so he would be proud of me. I remember being twenty-two years old and terrified to tell him that I got a speeding ticket. It took me years to realize that my dad loved me simply because I was his daughter, not because I was good at what I did or because I never broke any rules.

Even when they do not show it, your parents love you and want God's best for your life. I spoke recently with a mom who was considering sending her daughter out of the country in an exchange-student program. She thought it would open up a world of new opportunities for her daughter. This mom's intentions were good, but her daughter misunderstood them. She felt like her mom was trying to get rid of her so she could focus more time on her other "more perfect" daughter.

Forgive and Forget

Many times, when dealing with our parents, we have to look past our own feelings and try to understand where they are coming from. We need to make an extra effort to look for good *intentions* even when their *methods* may not be the best. And in all parent/child relationships, we need to learn to let go of the past. If we don't, it can be extremely destructive to each of us as individuals and for the relationship as a whole.

When I was young, my parents separated for a year. Eventually my dad came home and, thankfully, my parents reconciled. Even during the time they were apart, though, I saw my dad regularly.

But almost twenty years after my dad had returned home, I realized I still harbored bitterness toward him for leaving. I always loved my dad, and we were close. But there was an underlying pain that was never healed in me. Because that time of separation was never talked about, the wound was never allowed to heal. Eventually its effects—a lack of trust and inner pain—nearly destroyed other relationships in my life.

I finally got to a place where I *had to talk openly* with both of my parents about it and let God heal my heart. I had to make myself vulnerable and face a few things I didn't want to face. But being open and honest put me on a path to healing that I didn't even know was possible.

If one or both of your parents (or stepparents) have hurt you through divorce, remarriage, cutting words, or another incident, you need to do a thorough heart check to make sure you have truly forgiven them. If not, you are slowly and silently destroying *yourself*. Someone once told me that to test whether you have truly forgiven someone, ask yourself if you still feel compelled to talk about what that person did to hurt you. If you are still talking about it, you're not over it. If you're still thinking about it, you're not over it.

Do not let bitterness or miscommunication rob you of a peaceful and rewarding relationship with one or both of your parents. None of us is perfect. We will all hurt someone else at one time or another in our lives. We are all saved by grace, and we are all allowed to experience lasting relationships with other people by grace as well. Don't be a grace killer in your relationships.

R-E-S-P-E-C-T: FIND OUT WHAT IT MEANS TO ... YOUR PARENTS

A third definition that the dictionary gives for *honor* is "high respect, as shown for special merit; esteem." Being a parent is the toughest, and most important, job anyone can and will ever have. And it should be treated as such. But all too often, we mock our parents' authority, and we defy and disobey them out of sheer rebellion.

They ask us to clean our rooms and we refuse. They tell us not to wear a certain outfit and we try to leave the house in it anyway. We are not allowed to watch certain movies at home, so we go to our friend's house and watch them. What we fail to realize is that God knows what we are doing and He is clear about what He expects from those who follow Him. He insists that we must respect *our parents' authority* in our lives, even when we claim we cannot respect *them*.

By choosing to disregard this command, we are not only disobeying our parents, but we are also disobeying God, since He put our parents over us for this very purpose. Unless your parents have asked you to do something clearly against His will, *God is going to take their side* if you choose to take it up with Him.

That stinks, I know. Trust me, I really know. I have had my own fair share of moments when I did not want to obey my parents' rules or abide by their decisions. I'm strong willed and independent; it was hard for me to realize that I didn't really have a choice in any of it. I wasn't the parent, so the decision wasn't mine. They will stand accountable to God for their decisions and actions, and we will stand accountable to God for ours. So we cannot waste time worrying about them, because it is not going to get us anywhere—at least, not anywhere productive.

I know many girls who get bent out of shape over not being allowed to date or watch certain movies. Some are infuriated with their parents because of curfews and other rules. As unjust as some of these things may seem, it is still God's command to you to obey your parents, even when you think their rules are pointless or ridiculous.

We are responsible for our own actions and for how we choose to interact with other people. We know what God has called us to do—honor our parents—and part of that honor is to obey them. The next time one of your parents asks you to do something, make a conscious effort to drop whatever else you are doing and do it right away. Don't ask questions. Don't offer excuses. Don't tell them to wait.

Most likely you will find that the more respect you give to your parents, the more respect they will give to you. If you honor their requests, they will see that you are responsible and can be trusted, and it is probably safe to say that with more trust will come more responsibility and potentially even more freedom.

No matter who your parents are, whether they are Christians or non-Christians (or one of each), you can be assured that *God handpicked them just for you* with specific purposes in mind. Acts 17:26 says that God appointed the very time and place in which each of us would live. It is safe to assume that your placement in your particular family was His divine appointment as well.

They Know More Than You Think

It is also important to note that your parents are not as dumb as you think they are. At least 90 percent of the time, when my parents have given me advice in my adult life, they have been right. They were probably mostly right throughout my childhood and teen years as well. The difference is that now I covet the advice I used to so angrily despise.

Now I covet the advice I used to so angrily despise.

Many times our parents have learned from their mistakes and would like to impart a portion of their wisdom to us in order to prevent heartache in our own lives. And although our situations may be different, the principles and theories behind them remain the same. We would be wise to learn from both what our parents have done right and what they have done wrong.

Sometimes the things we fight about are downright stupid. In junior high I really wanted to wear makeup. My mom was fine with that, but she wasn't fine with the *amount* of makeup I wanted to wear. I liked to layer it on thick and dark—I wanted the dramatic look. I used to get furious with my mom over this. I wouldn't even give her a chance to show me what looked good and what didn't. She wanted to take me to a department store makeup counter to have my colors done, and I stubbornly wanted my drugstore brands that were *not* my colors and made my skin break out.

Looking back at old pictures, I cringe when I see how right she was. I am glad she allowed me and my friend Krissy to take a modeling class where we at least learned something about choosing makeup colors and products wisely. I would have saved myself a lot of time, effort, and pimples had I just listened to her in the first place.

The next time you find yourself arguing with one of your parents, ask yourself these questions: "Is this really worth fighting about? Is this argument really necessary? Is it going to get us anywhere? What am I trying to accomplish here?" If you don't have good answers to these questions, give up. Some things are just not worth the effort we put into them.

A professor I had in college used to say, "Pick the hill you want to die on." He meant that you needed to seriously consider the battles—how important they were—before you engaged in them. Most of the time, if we thought through our arguments with our parents, we wouldn't really want to argue with them—about those things, anyway. Apply a simple rule here: Think before you speak. Trust me, it works wonders.

ABOVE ALL ELSE, LOVE THEM

You are commanded to honor your parents. And true honor always brings love with it. A good rule of thumb in determining how you should interact with your parents is simply this. Open your Bible to 1 Corinthians 13 and go through verses four through seven, inserting your name wherever the words *love* or *charity* appear. "_____ is patient, _____ is kind, _____ is not jealous. . . ." See if you really act in that manner toward your parents.

Are you patient with your working mother when she doesn't always get dinner on the table right at six? Are you kind to your dad even when you feel as if he has not acknowledged you in weeks? Are you jealous of a stepparent or sibling who gets more attention from your dad or mom than you do? There will be days when loving your parents is hard, but it does not mean you can give up and quit.

It is important to remember that our parents are people, and they have feelings. Our words and our actions have the potential to hurt and scar them, just like their words and actions have the potential to hurt and scar us. We must never use rebellion and withholding love as weapons in our relationship with our parents. We must never maliciously try to manipulate them or make them feel like failures. Those behaviors do not fit into the category of honoring our parents. The bottom line is simply this: According to God's Word, any time we choose to dishonor our parents, we are in the wrong. So let's work at getting this one right and honor them in every way possible. Let's lead others with our example of what the word *honor* really means.

FOR FURTHER THOUGHT:

1. How would you describe your relationship with each of your parents?

2. What areas do you and your parents tend to fight about most? Why do you think that is?

3. What are some ways you are "performing" to gain their love?

4. What are ways you have honored your parents in the past? How did they respond?

5. What are some practical ways you can honor your parents right now?

LEADERSHIP IN ACTION:

Think of a mark, a token, or a gesture of respect that you can give to each of your parents. Go out of your way to do something out of the ordinary—ask your dad on a date; invite your mom out for a day of shopping and hanging out. Or offer to wash the car, do the dishes, or watch a younger sibling so your mom or dad has some time to relax. Make each of your parents feel valued and honored. And do not ask for anything in return for your kind gesture.

10

Outlive Yourself

He was a dreamer. Everyone knew it and laughed him off. But one day his dreams changed; suddenly they weren't anything to laugh about. Joseph, the eleventh of Jacob's twelve sons—and the first of his two sons with Jacob's favorite wife, Rachel—came to his family and told them he had dreamed that one day they would bow before him. From that day forward, his brothers didn't like him anymore. It was bad enough he was Daddy's favorite, but now he was exalting himself, and that just was not cool.

So they sold him into slavery and told their father that Joseph was dead. Their plan seemed to work perfectly at first. The only problem was that Joseph's dream was not just any dream—it was a vision from God. Although he had to endure being a slave, being falsely accused of rape, and spending years in prison for a crime he did not commit while he watched other prisoners (who *were* guilty) go free, God was building the character of a leader in him.

When God first gave him the dream, Joseph was much too cocky to live it out. He hadn't yet learned that a true leader does not go around boasting about the position God has bestowed upon him or her. So God gave Joseph a small glimpse of what He wanted Joseph's life to be, but before raising him up to the highest of heights, He took him down into the lowest of lows.

When Joseph was finally ready, God made the dream a reality; Joseph's family *did* come and bow before him without realizing who he was. And in gracious humility, he forgave them for selling him into slavery, because he saw that the thing he would have never chosen for himself was the one thing that God used to make his dream, God's vision, become a reality.

Don't get me wrong. I am sure there were days Joseph thought his vision was just a stupid dream. There may have been times where he thought it would never happen. But Joseph the dreamer dared to trust the God who dreams, and his life became more than he could ever have imagined.

Sometimes God comes to us as He did to Joseph and gives us a vision—or a small glimpse—of what He wants our lives to be. He allows us to hold on to that vision, and He sets it ahead of us like a mile marker or goal we must reach.

Perhaps God has given you a vision for a life lived as a foreign missionary, a school teacher, a social worker, a recording artist, an author, or an actress. Maybe you think your dreams are out of your reach. *Your* dreams may be, but *God's* dreams never are. As a Christian girl in today's society, you have the power to change the world around you. You have more of an influence than you can even imagine, and with God's power you will be able to step up and change your generation.

Hopefully this book has served as a tool to remind you that you do not have to do something, say something, buy something, or be something just because everyone else tells you that you need to do, say, buy, or be those things.

But I also hope that your glimpse of God's vision for your life does not stop there. His collective vision for each of our lives is that we would glorify Him through all we say and all we do. He desires to see us change the world through making wise choices and standing for what is right when everything around us is all wrong.

There is more to it than that, though. God has also given each of us individual passions and talents like we talked about earlier (remember your SHAPE?). And when we combine His collective vision for mankind with His personal vision for our lives, we have a glimpse of the legacy He desires each of us to leave behind.

God desires for us, His daughters, to outlive ourselves. He desires for each of us to be a part of something that will live longer than we will. The only way we can do that is by pouring into other people. You may be young, but you still have countless opportunities to pour into people who are younger than you, the same age as you, and sometimes even older than you—all for the glory of God. So *let your life speak.*

Recently I sent an e-mail off to one of my former college professors, thanking her for some of the biblical principles she taught in her class. It's been years since I have taken the class, but I realized how often I use the things I learned in her class. So I wanted to take the opportunity to thank her for outliving herself. Her life greatly impacted mine, and certain ideas, words, and phrases that appear in my books were first learned in her classroom.

Legacy sparks the domino effect—when you line dominoes up in a circle and knock one over, the rest fall over one by one until every domino is touching the one in front of it and the one behind it. In much the same way we are to learn from those who come before us and lead those who come after us. So what about you? What elements make up your legacy?

WHY VISION IS VITAL

For those of us who aspire to be leaders, vision is vitally important. Without it, we will surely give up long before we have reached our goals. Even more importantly, we will give up before we have reached *God's* goals for us. Proverbs 29:18 (KJV) says, "Where there is no vision, the people perish." Dying young, or having our dreams die while we are still young, is not an appealing thought.

As I was growing up I had many aspirations. I wanted to be an actress, I wanted to be a model, and I wanted to be a singer. But of all the dreams I ever had, there was one that stuck. No matter what happened, it's what I always came back to . . . writing.

I wanted to write. And although God took that vision and reshaped it over the years (I went from wanting to be a political speech writer, to a Pulitzer Prize–winning journalist, to finally resting on being an author of Christian books), I could never have made that dream a reality without three things: God's grace, God's guidance, and God's vision for my life.

You see, God is the author of vision. Many times He is the one who gives us vision in the first place. His visions for our lives are usually huge and magnificent. We are the ones who diminish them, not the other way around. God's *purposes* in giving us these dreams, however, may be quite different than our own.

Remember, God has a *ministry* for you in His church and a *mission* for you in the world.[1] His vision for your life will encompass both of those things. Sometimes our dreams for our lives don't include either. My childhood dreams of becoming an actress, model, or singer were all about *my* glory. They weren't about God.

I'm not saying He cannot use people in those industries; I'm simply saying that none of these aspirations were *my* calling. God saw me better suited to serve Him somewhere else. I could have wasted a lot of years arguing with Him, but instead I chose to let Him readjust my vision and give me a new perspective. Like an eye doctor who gives out prescriptions that help people to see more clearly, sometimes God needs to tweak things just a bit so we can better see His will for us.

THE GOD WHO LETS US SEE

Out of all of the dreams you have ever had, there is probably one that stands out above all the rest. In your mind you have a picture of what you would do if you could do anything at all. Like a crown that is held just above your head, that dream hangs in the heavens just waiting for you to grow into it.[2] You can see it, but you cannot touch it yet.

Being able to see that dream, that crown, is vision. If you can see it and believe it's possible, you will be willing to work for it. You will be willing to sacrifice and grow in order to obtain it. That crown is your goal, and if you can see it, you are already halfway there. So if you have a dream, a vision God has given you for your life, don't close your eyes and shut it out just because it seems so far away. It may be out of your grasp, but it certainly is not outside of God's.

Ephesians 3:20 tells us that we serve a God who can do "exceedingly abundantly above all that we ask or think" (NKJV). Many times He gives us just a glimpse of what the exceeding abundantly above will be if we will simply let Him work out *His* plans for our lives. Our problem, though, is that we aren't satisfied to just see the vision; we want to touch it.

Maybe you don't seem to be reaching your crown today because you are not quite ready to handle all that comes with it. Maybe you are like my four-year-old friend "Lucy" who tries to cheat and get on the Disneyland rides she is too short for by wearing what she calls "big honkin' shoes." Maybe you come to God trying to claim that you are ready to receive your crown, and you walk away discouraged when He refuses to give it to you. Like the people who run Disneyland rides know what ages are appropriate for riding them, so God knows when you are mature enough to handle the vision for your life. Stop trying to tell God you are ready, and simply let Him *make* you ready for your crown. He'll know the right time for your "crowning," and He won't hold back when it comes.

David's Path to the Throne

Look at what He had to do in the life of King David. Anointed as Israel's next king at a young age, David was forced to travel a path that took him from the pastures, to the battlefield, to the palace of another king, and into the back hills fleeing for his life before he was ever allowed to touch his crown. David knew God's anointing rested on him. He knew what he was made to do. But there were some things God had to do in David's heart before David was ready to wear his crown.

If God has given you a vision for your life, it will be bigger than anything you can do on your own. At a conference I attended recently, Lori Salierno said, "If your vision is small enough for you to handle on your own, it is not big enough for God." She also said, "God will take you to the edge, and if He doesn't come through, you're dead meat. That's how you know you are living in His vision for your life."

Let Him prepare you for your crown.

His vision for your life is about His glory, so you can rest assured that He will *always* come through for us in fulfilling *His* vision for our lives. It's really only our selfish prayers that go unanswered. God will not shortchange us, so give Him time. Let Him prepare you for your crown, like He did David. And when you are ready, you can rest assured that He will gladly place it on your head and you will find that it fits just right.

PICTURE PERFECT

Perhaps you hold the picture of what your life could be in your mind like a photograph. Thinking about it makes your heart race with excitement. Actually doing it causes a lump to grow in your throat. Quickly and quietly you push that dream aside, either burying it in the secret chambers of your heart or filing it away in the back of your mind. Every now and then you pull it out and look at it longingly, but as your heart races and your throat closes, you put it away again and settle back down in a place called *reality*.

Many times the things we thought we could never do are the very things God has called us to do. Usually God has bigger dreams for us than we have for ourselves, so we should be going to Him to ask what it is He would have us do. We need to ask Him for *His* picture for our lives. Chances are, it will somehow involve that very thing we so desperately want to do.

God graciously allows me to write, although not in the way I initially thought I would. Our dreams and God's dreams usually align only when we are seeking Him, because as we seek Him we allow Him to *change us* as He unfolds His plan. God's plan for us will always result in His glory. So it is important that we look at our dreams in light of that and examine whether the glory will be His or ours if we pursue them.

Different Dreams for Different Girls

The dreams God gives us are not always what we would consider spiritual. Many times they are very practical ways He will use our gifts and talents for His glory. In high school I knew several girls with dreams. I can think of three who are actively living those dreams out today.

One is a high-school basketball coach who works toward making a difference in the lives of her players. She doesn't just teach them about the sport—she teaches them about life. Another girl from my high school is an elementary school teacher in a low-income school. She spends five days a week investing in students who don't have much materially, but they are made rich by her wholehearted devotion to them. And the third girl is a junior high and high school life-skills counselor who helps kids to reach their dreams by developing the skills they will need to get there.

To these girls the things they are doing are not just jobs; they are callings. God gave them a passion and a vision years ago that they would one day make a difference in the lives of others in these capacities. They worked hard in school and volunteered in churches and the community for years in order to get where they are today. But the lives they live today are a result of *living out* the vision God gave them years ago.

What is the vision God has given you? Is there something that excites you like nothing else in this world? Do you have something that makes you pound your fist on the table with enthusiasm when you talk about it? If nothing comes to mind at the moment, simply pray the same prayer the apostle Paul prayed when he was apprehended by the Lord on the road to Damascus. "Lord, what do You want me to do?" (Acts 9:6 NKJV). Chances are, He has been waiting for you to ask so He can answer that question for you. God does have a vision for your life, and if you seek Him, He will be more than willing to let you in on it.

VISION KEEPS THE FIRE BURNING

Vision is what keeps us going when we want to give up. It's even what kept Jesus going in His darkest hour. Hebrews 12:2 tells us that Jesus endured the cross for the *joy* set before Him. That joy was God's vision of mankind being able to enter into eternity with Him because of Christ's atoning sacrifice.

BEING A GIRL WHO LEADS

But living in that vision was not easy in the Garden of Gethsemane or when Jesus stood before Pilate. And there is no way it was easy as He was beaten, mocked, and eventually crucified. Mark chapter 15 tells us that people passed by Him hurling insults, telling Him if He really was the Son of God, to come off the cross and save himself.

He looked ahead and saw the end result.

Jesus could have come off the cross that day, but instead He looked ahead and saw the end result of what He was doing. Eternity with you was enough to keep Him there.

In our own lives we will have moments when the visions of the great things God wants us to do become threatened. There will be those who doubt us, those who question our motives, and those who hurl downright abuse in our faces. But we have to keep living in the vision God has given us.

When I first set out to write a book, my friends and family laughed. When they saw how serious I was, a few of them began to support me. Others still thought I was a dreamer with my head in the clouds. I had to keep pressing on toward the vision God had for me even when others thought it was ridiculous.

Luke 1:37 tells us that nothing is impossible with God. It is extremely important we hold on to this truth when our vision is threatened and our faith is tried. A big part of having vision is knowing that God is working on your behalf even when you cannot see what He is doing. It's being able to sit in prison like Joseph and hang on the cross like Jesus and say, "But God told me ... and I believe it."

It's been said that "you have never tested God's resources until you have attempted the impossible."[3] Sometimes God uses our reality to make our vision seem impossible simply so *we will trust Him more*. Other times, He does it so that when the fulfillment of the vision comes, we won't be able to boast in our own strength. We'll have to say, "It only happened because God did it."

But that does not mean we should not do our part to prepare for the vision God has given us for our lives. I told you earlier I kept journals and taught a small girls' Bible study when God first showed me He was going to use me to write books and speak to large groups. My friends went to school and worked hard to get to places where they could teach and coach. A lot of times God must prepare you to live out His vision for your life. He must train you for your task. What is He training you for in this moment?

The Prayer of a Leader

Leroy Eims once said, "A leader is one who sees more than others see, who sees farther than others see, and who sees before others see."[4] If we truly aspire to be girls who lead, we need to ask God to allow us to see *more* than others see, *farther* than others see, and *before* others see. In essence, we need to ask the Lord to give us vision—His vision for our lives.

Without vision our lives count for nothing. Without vision we will surely perish. I have watched too many people I know have a dream for their life only to give up on it halfway through or not even attempt to live it out at all. These people walk around defeated most of the time. They have no sense of purpose. Vision gives us purpose. It gives us a sense of calling in life. It gives us a reason for living. It gives us a chance to outlive ourselves.

If we have vision and purpose, we will eventually catch the attention of others because in the end, that is what we all seek. And once you have the attention of those around you, *they will want to follow you*. And if they are willing to follow you, you will be able to lead them to the Creator of your vision and the Maker of your purpose. In doing so, you will be able to use your God-given vision for God's glory. There is no privilege greater than that.

Lessons From the Blind

I would venture to say that the girl who chooses not to see is no better than the girl who cannot see. If you lack vision and you choose not to ask God for it, then you might as well be blind. Imagine living your life in total darkness. You can see nothing but pitch black before you at all times. There is no light or dark, there is no beauty to behold. In a sense, it is like living in a world where nothing really exists. You can hear things and feel things, but you can never see things. As bad as that all sounds, someone once asked Helen Keller if there was anything worse than being blind.

She admitted that there was one thing: being able to see but having no vision. How is it that a girl who lived in total blackness could see more than those of us who have twenty-twenty vision? Helen Keller got it. Being able to see may get you through today, but *having vision will get you through the rest of your life.*

I grew up hearing the phrase, "It's like the blind leading the blind," thrown around casually. But in college I interned at a nearby community college where there were a significant number of blind students. And I will never forget the first time I ever saw the blind lead the blind.

With tears in my eyes, I watched one student with a walking stick lead another without one. Holding the person by the arm, she spoke as she directed. The two moved very slowly, and people helped them by staying out of their way. I remember thinking it would have been easier for them if I had gone over to help, since I could see where they were going, but I didn't want to risk offending them by interfering. Slowly, and surely, the girls got to their destination.

I am eternally grateful that we serve a God who is not afraid of "interfering" in our lives. Without Him we are all just like the blind leading the blind. And just like those two girls I observed that day, we stumble around in darkness, moving very, very slowly and never really making it farther than a few steps at a time.

How much quicker (and farther) we would be able to go if only we would allow the Lord to give us His vision! We cannot see where we are going in life, but God can. And if we let Him take us by the hand, we will get there with a lot less pain and frustration.

Let's stop letting the blind lead the blind and ask the Lord for new eyes with which to see. With His vision guiding us, let's rise up and become girls who lead.

FOR FURTHER THOUGHT:

1. Do you have a vision you feel the Lord has given you for your life? What is it? If not, how can you go about seeking the Lord for such vision?

2. List five things you desire to do with your life. How many of them involve having a mission to the world and a ministry to the church? Are they for your glory or God's?

3. Name an example of someone in your life who has vision. How is he or she living out that vision?

4. Name someone in your life who has no vision. How do you think he or she is "perishing" as a result?

5. Describe a time when your vision has been threatened and you had to hang on tight in order to avoid giving up.

LEADERSHIP IN ACTION:

Find a new way you can "live in the vision" God has given you for your life. If you sing, find a new way to use that for God's glory. If you play sports or work well with children, use those things in a new way. Whatever it is, take one step closer to fulfilling that vision. Don't let your age or your busy schedule get in your way. After all, what good is vision if you don't use it?

Notes

1. Rick Warren, *The Purpose Driven Life* (Grand Rapids: Zondervan, 2002), 229.
2. Concept taken from Carol Kent's *Becoming a Woman of Influence* (Colorado Springs: NavPress, 1999), 152.
3. John Maxwell, *The Journey From Success to Significance* (Nashville: J. Countryman, 2004), 104.
4. Ibid., 106.

Epilogue

Being a girl who leads isn't about being in a ministry or in a labeled leadership role. It's about how you live your life. The world is full of followers—and our generation is perishing as a result.

But God has given you the power to be the change the world so desperately needs to see. It won't be easy. And it isn't a one-time task. Being a girl who leads is a daily, moment-by-moment decision to stand up for what is right and forsake what is wrong—no matter the cost.

In a world that is compromising in everything from what movies they watch to what their sexual preferences are, a girl who boldly stands for what is right will emerge as a leader due to one simple fact—she's *not* following.

After reading this book, you are now equipped with many different ways to quit following and start leading. You have been given the tools to become a wiser consumer who refuses to buy into trends that stand out in stark contrast to God's glory. You have been challenged to choose your friends wisely as you have seen what kind of an effect those you choose to associate with usually have on you.

You have been challenged to be authentic and be yourself—leaving all of your masks at the door. And you and I have both been called on the carpet for the compromises we make in our vocabularies and how others will perceive us based on the words we use. We have discussed the importance of having boundary lines that we abide by and live within.

Together we have also uncovered the mystery of what it means to guard our hearts—and why it is so important. We've been taught how to hold our tongues when they want to run away from us and how to check ourselves for gossip. We've been grossed out by the thought of being a dirty Band-Aid, and we've been challenged to truly honor our parents—not just obey them begrudgingly. And we've been encouraged to take all of these truths and outlive ourselves, creating a lasting legacy for Christ and His kingdom.

Like I said in the introduction, this book has the power to change the world if every girl who reads it applies its truth wholeheartedly to her life. You cannot account for the crowd, but you can account for yourself. You've read the book.... What are you going to do with what you've read?

My prayer is that you step out and change the world and truly embrace the concept of being a girl who leads.

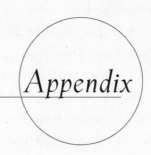

Appendix

WHICH SPIRITUAL GIFT IS YOURS?

The Bible tells us that God chooses at least one spiritual gift for every individual. It's something He gives you—not exclusively, of course—that you will delight in using. Paul describes most of these gifts in Romans 12:6–8; 1 Corinthians 12:7–10, 28; and Ephesians 4:11–13. Read the definitions, then check the gift(s) listed below that you may have.

Gifts in Romans:

_____ *Prophecy:* hearing a special "right now" message from God and speaking it to His people.

_____ *Serving:* recognizing jobs that need to be done and finding a way to complete them.

_____ *Teaching:* communicating information (by word and deed) so others can understand and grow.

_____ *Exhortation:* speaking words that encourage others and stimulate their faith.

_____ *Giving:* cheerfully and generously sharing what you have with others.

_____ *Leading:* catching God's vision, setting goals, and influencing others to help reach them.

_____ *Mercy:* genuinely feeling what others are feeling, then being sympathetic, comforting, and kind.

Gifts in 1 Corinthians:

_____ *Wisdom:* using insight from the Holy Spirit to give wise advice right when it is needed.

_____ *Knowledge:* discovering, understanding, and clarifying information to help God's people.

_____ *Faith:* having unquenchable trust and confidence about God's plan and purposes.

_____ *Healing:* laying hands on an ill person, praying for them, and seeing God cure them.

_____ *Miracles:* serving as the human instrument that receives God's power to perform powerful acts.

_____ *Distinguishing of spirits:* knowing if a person's spirit is from God or Satan.

_____ *Speaking in tongues:* receiving and delivering a message from God through a divine language you have never learned. Also used in one's private prayer to God.

_____ *Interpreting tongues:* receiving from God the translation of a message given in tongues.

_____ *Prophecy:* same as on previous page.

Gifts in Ephesians:

_____ *Apostle:* gathering believers together in a new environment.

_____ *Evangelism:* sharing the good news of Jesus and winning non-believers to Him.

_____ *Pastoring:* providing care and spiritual feeding to benefit God's people.

_____ *Prophecy and Teaching:* same as previous mentions.

Here are a few more spiritual gifts mentioned in other places in Scripture:

_____ *Celibacy:* remaining single and sexually abstinent for purposes of serving God (1 Corinthians 7:7–8).

_____ *Hospitality:* welcoming into your home those who need food and/or lodging (1 Peter 4:9).

_____ *Intercession:* praying on behalf of others, standing in the gap (Colossians 1:9–12).

_____ *Exorcism:* casting out demons using God's supernatural power (Acts 16:16–18).

_____ *Helps:* working behind the scenes to assist others in fulfilling their ministry (Romans 16:1–2).

_____ *Administration:* creating a plan and organizing others to complete it (Titus 1:5).[1]

Notes

1. Andrea Stephens, *Girlfriend, You Are A B.A.B.E.!* (Grand Rapids, MI: Revell) 2005, 127–128. *www.andreastephens.com*

Are you willing to answer the call?

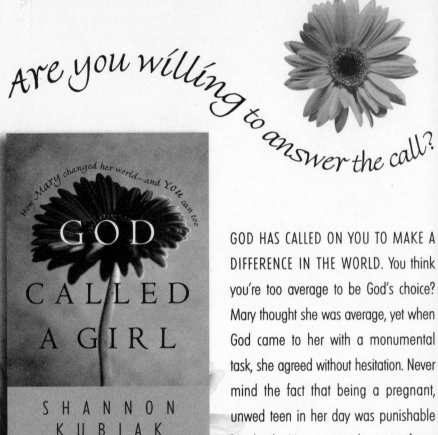

GOD HAS CALLED ON YOU TO MAKE A DIFFERENCE IN THE WORLD. You think you're too average to be God's choice? Mary thought she was average, yet when God came to her with a monumental task, she agreed without hesitation. Never mind the fact that being a pregnant, unwed teen in her day was punishable by death. Mary, a simple, insignificant girl, was just a teenager when she revolutionized society and changed the world. God is looking for world changers. God has big plans for your life; see what He can do with just one person fully committed to Him.

God Called A Girl by Shannon Kubiak